MILTON'S
PARADISE LOST

SYDNEY STUDIES IN LITERATURE

FOUNDING EDITOR (1965-7): the late Professor K. G. W. Cross, then Head of the English Department, University of Newcastle

GENERAL EDITORS (1967-   ): G. A. Wilkes, Challis Professor of English Literature and Dr A. P. Riemer, Senior Lecturer in English Literature, University of Sydney

MILTON'S

PARADISE LOST

MICHAEL WILDING
Senior Lecturer in English
University of Sydney

SYDNEY UNIVERSITY PRESS

SYDNEY UNIVERSITY PRESS

Press Building, University of Sydney

First published 1969

Copyright 1969 Text and Bibliography by Michael Wilding

National Library of Australia registry number AUS 68-2277
Library of Congress Catalog Card Number 68-21935
SBN 424 05850 2

This book is supported by money from
THE ELEANOR SOPHIA WOOD BEQUEST

Printed in Australia
at The Griffin Press, Adelaide
and registered in Australia for transmission by post as a book

CONTENTS

To my mother and father

PREFACE

The volume of critical and scholarly studies dealing with Milton increases inexorably year by year. Adding to this mass of material needs explanation, and I offer two tentative defences. An introductory study can offer some assistance to the reader confronted by the daunting range of commentary—offer some indication of the questions being asked and the sorts of answers being proposed; and indicate especially the new questions being asked in the revival of critical interest in *Paradise Lost* over the last fifteen years. (Consequently I have dealt with the major critics of *Paradise Lost* not only in the final chapter specifically about the critics, but throughout this study.) A very new Milton is being offered to us now. Much of the newness lies in the recognition of his complexity— the richness and subtlety of his verse, the intellectual rigorousness of his argument. This newly rediscovered Milton is one who invites commentary, discussion, argument. This is my second defence. Milton's claim 'to justifie the wayes of God to men' was a huge and challenging one: it is intended to engage our attention, our combative intelligence. *Paradise Lost* is not the Bible, Milton is not God: our response is not to be one of passive adoration and acceptance. Milton's aim is not to praise or celebrate God's ways, but to justify them: it is because for him they can be justified—intellectually, morally—that they can then be praised and celebrated. And so we should read the poem with our full intelligence, treating the arguments as arguments, provocative of a dialectic and interchange with the reader. And the justification comes not only from the logical structure of the presented issues, but from the verse. *Paradise Lost* is a poem, not a prose commentary. The verse requires the same rigorous attention from us as the case it is presenting, for if the verse fails, the case fails too. The verse demands our analytic attention, and always rewards it. It is a mark of the richness of the verse that we can keep asking questions of it, that it is never exhausted; questions about the relevance of an image here, an incident there, are questions that need to be asked, and that lead us to answers involving the great argument. I hope some sense of the

7

tautness of the poem's structure, the interdependence of the poem's argument, narrative, and verse, emerges at the end of this study.

I have incorporated occasional sentences and paragraphs from reviews and articles I originally contributed to *Balcony*, *Essays in Criticism*, *Melbourne Critical Review*, and *Modern Language Review*, and acknowledgement is gratefully made to the editors of those journals. As an undergraduate I was fortunate to be taught by Dennis H. Burden, Christopher Ricks, and W. W. Robson; to their teaching then and their published studies of Milton since I am immensely indebted; and to the founding editor of this series, the late K. G. W. Cross, I am grateful for encouragement and lively and valuable discussions.

All quotations from *Paradise Lost* are from the text of *Milton's Poems*, edited by B. A. Wright (Everyman's Library, 1959—J. M. Dent, London, E. P. Dutton, New York). Quotations from Milton's prose works have generally been taken from *Milton's Prose Writings*, introduction by K. M. Burton (Everyman's Library, revised edition, 1958). This is designated as 'Burton' in the notes.

University of Sydney
February 1969

Michael Wilding

CHAPTER I

An Approach to the Poem

The heroic poem, Dryden wrote in 1697, is 'undoubtedly the greatest work which the soul of man is capable to perform'.[1] The idea was a commonplace, but actual epic poems in English were not. Despite his disillusion with England in the failure of the Commonwealth, and in the restoration of the monarchy, Milton still had enough patriotic as well as personal ambition to attempt to provide this necessary pinnacle to a nation's literature. He chose, moreover, to write in English, although the Renaissance argument as to whether the vernacular languages were suitable for an epic persisted. After all, Milton had written propaganda for the Commonwealth in Latin, as well as Latin verse, and *Paradise Lost* was later translated into Latin by Henry Bold. Yet he chose to write in English. To write an epic in the vernacular was to prove the vernacular. 'There ought no regard be sooner had than to God's glory, by the honour and instruction of my country', he wrote in *The Reason of Church Government* (1641), so he planned

to fix all the industry and art I could unite to the adorning of my native tongue; not to make verbal curiosities the end (that were a toilsome vanity), but to be an interpreter and relater of the best and sagest things among mine own citizens throughout this island in the mother dialect. That, what the greatest and choicest wits of Athens, Rome, or modern Italy, and those Hebrews of old did for their country, I, in my proportion, with this over and above, of being a Christian, might do for mine; not caring to be once named abroad, though perhaps I could attain to that, but content with these British islands as my world.[2]

Despite his political disillusionment, this patriotism remained with him.

Although there was little English precedent, except perhaps Spenser's *Faerie Queene*, for Milton to follow in his epic, the classical tradition was clear enough. Almost all the traditional features of

1. John Dryden (ed. W. P. Ker, 1900), *Works*, II.154.
2. Burton, p. 352.

epic are included in *Paradise Lost*: the beginning in the middle of the action, the visit to the underworld, the vision of the future, the invocations, the encyclopaedic range of information, epic epithets, lists (in the second edition Milton added three more lines to the list of diseases—XI.485-487), and single combat fights. The epic was a long-established and self-consciously literary form, and Milton carefully followed, and exploited for his particular purposes, its conventions. C. S. Lewis in *A Preface to Paradise Lost* valuably establishes this literary background.

But Milton was not a simple follower of the conventions. His material presented special problems, and *Paradise Lost* is an original, innovatory work, not a scholarly reconstruction of classical epic. The remark of C. S. Lewis, for instance, that Milton 'is writing epic poetry which is a species of narrative poetry'[3] needs to be questioned. Milton's interest in narrative is very different from Homer's. There was not much need for Milton to present a narrative of the events he chose. It was already there in the Bible, and the story was so well known as to make it difficult for him to employ any of the natural qualities of narrative—surprise and suspense. Donald Davie has argued that Milton's elaborate syntax 'is employed characteristically to check narrative impetus and frustrate musical pleasure'.[4] He finds this a fault; yet if we argue that the interest of *Paradise Lost* is not one of linear narrative, the syntax might be seen as a great success. The poem could hardly succeed if it were organized primarily on a narrative principle, on the principle of asking 'What happens next?' We know what happens next, except with minor unbiblical features such as the Sin and Death allegory. Instead of a linear narrative, Milton has built a structure of cross-reference, parallelism, echo, parody, ironic prolepsis; the questions we ask are, 'What will be compared to what next, what will presage or re-enact what next?' Hence his great reliance on similes. Similes were traditional to epic, but Milton uses them not as digressions from a simple main action, but for a complex of comparisons and contrasts: the contrasts (how unlike . . .) are as important as the comparisons.

There is little narrative interest in the poem—Adam and Eve can only wait, doing nothing: God's foreseeing the Fall prevents any surprise we might have. Satan's preparation and carrying out of his campaign is the main narrative impulse, but this is deliberately frustrated by our seeing God's foreknowing events. Even the narrative of the war in Heaven is deliberately anti-narrative in manner: the pointlessness of the war of exactly equal combatants prevents our

3. C. S. Lewis, *A Preface to Paradise Lost* (1942), p. 1.
4. Frank Kermode (ed.), *The Living Milton* (1960), p. 83.

getting interest from 'What happens next?' Nothing new happens next, and the war might have gone on dully for ever like that.

The similes work by aggregation rather than linear development. The fallen angels are described as fallen leaves in Vallombrosa, and then as sedge floating on the Red Sea, which brings in a reference to the oppressors of the Israelites drowned in the Red Sea, and the angels are left finally implicitly compared to 'floating Carcasses / And broken Chariot Wheels' (I.310-311). Milton is achieving a montage effect, aiming not for linear development but for a multilateral image of contemporaneity. The angels are all these different things at the same time, and our evaluation of them depends on the complex of our moral and aesthetic evaluations of the differing objects to which they are compared. It is an aggregation of comparison made possible by the range of Milton's referents —the classical, Biblical and medieval worlds, literature, religion, myth, superstition, the modern world, technology, astronomy, architecture, voyaging, war, music and heroism. The Renaissance epic was to include all knowledge. Milton makes good use of this requirement for his other purposes.

One result is a qualification of the visual effects of the poem. It is not, as Eliot felt, that Milton had little visual imagination.[5] Rather, he presents not one but a complex of visual images. Some early film-makers tried this sort of thing—Gance's *Napoléon* has a threefold screen with a separate sequence of images on each section. In Milton's Hell, we have a montage of barren wastes, monotony, aridity (reminding us by contrast of the huge fertility and sweet interchange of Paradise); of burning lake, flying mountains, volcanoes; and of the grandiose magnificence of Pandæmonium and marching armies. Similarly Paradise is a complex of country-house, walled citadel, garden of love, domestic landscape with grazing flocks, like-unlike classical garden, idyllic pastoral world, nature's rich profusion, bejewelled artificiality. It is multi-faceted, with each detail vividly evoked sensually—sight, sound, smell; and further augmented by the referents of the similes. But each aspect is to be valued as a separate facet of the multi-form whole, rather than as subordinate to a single 'organic' image readily apprehensible in one visual unit. The complexity and recurrence of the Miltonic simile check the narrative of the poem and encourage the reader not to read on simply for the story, but to amass, to compare.

The interest is not merely in asking, 'Why is this event described by this image?' but, 'Why is this passage echoing—or prefiguring— this other event?' For instance, Satan rising from the burning lake

5. T. S. Eliot, 'Milton I' in *On Poetry and Poets* (1957), p. 139.

is compared to a mountain blown by subterranean wind (I.230ff.)—
so prefiguring the hills thrown in the war in Heaven. The structure
of echo and prolepsis here is complex. For the reader, the flying
hill in Book I (and the hills the devils throw in II.540) prefigure
the hills the devils throw in the war in Book VI. But for the devils
(since the poem has begun in the chronological middle) the flying
hills of Hell are a reminiscence or echo of their defeat in Heaven.
Whereas the reader is given a preview of the war in Heaven—so
that when he sees it he will see Hell (of which he has already read)
being created there—the devils are being reminded of their defeat
(as a tormenting memory) and are shown unable to escape from
re-enacting the incidents of their destructiveness that is also a
self-destruction. By this use of prolepsis and reminiscence in a
poem of disrupted chronology, Milton is deliberately frustrating a
merely narrative organization. Of course there is a narrative
(Satan's campaign) and there are patterns of narrative imagery
(Satan's sea-voyage similes): but Milton is striving for this great
static effect, a complex of parallel, cross-reference and parody (Sin
parodying the Trinity, the devils parodying Eve's creation), an
enactment of the timelessness of God and eternity.

   Paradise Lost can be seen, then, as a huge static construct, as a
complex metaphor. The fall of the angels is literal—they are
thrown over Heaven's battlements; the fall of Adam is metaphoric—
though he lies prone as if fallen (X.580). The image of the physical
fall supplies a metaphor for the moral fall for both the devils and
man; the two falls are involved in each other by this parallel
metaphor, and also by their intertwined action: Satan's fall is a
sub-plot that is proleptic of Adam's, yet a metaphoric prolepsis
that turns into action since Satan contrives man's fall, and contrives
it because he is fallen. The pattern of falls is cyclic, each revolution
of the cycle connected with the next, suggesting man's continual
propensity to fall, to sin, until the final redemption ends the process.
Throughout we are reminded of the Fall—in simile (the angels like
fallen leaves, that have naturally fallen in the Fall, the seventeenth-
century word for Autumn), in flashback (Mulciber's fall), in action;
and in accretions to the whole range of vocabulary—high-low-
deep-depth-descend-rise-climb.

   Epic poetry traditionally has verbal repetition: the repeated
phrases derive from the oral basis of the heroic and epic—bards
had set phrases to aid improvisation in their spontaneous composi-
tion, and to aid memory. Milton uses the repetitions for his own
purposes of pointed parallelism and cross-reference—and so we
find the continual recurrence and play on words like fruit, fall and
light. Hence there is the continual tragic irony: after Adam and

Eve have eaten the fruit 'they in mutual accusation spent / The fruitless hours' (IX.1187-1188). The pun is both satirical and tragic. Such verbal play and repetition is basic to Milton's method.

Parody, irony—both linguistically, and in the larger structures such as the attempt to make Hell like Heaven and our realization of how it is both so different and distant and yet also so grotesquely a parody of it—these were methods especially appealing to the satirical—as Aubrey described him—Milton. They were especially appealing to the Milton who had gone blind when writing propaganda for the new society in which he had such faith, and which he felt his countrymen betrayed by the Restoration. The tragic ironies he drew out of the stories of Satan and Adam, of those two throwing away their own Paradises, were something he could treat after his own experiences. There is no need to see him as embittered—there is no evidence that he was. He seems to have achieved a sort of resignation. Paradise, after all, is not for this Earth—yet so nearly it might have been. The tragic fact of its loss is a theme suited to his own loss—of sight, of Christ's Kingdom on Earth: but the promise of its eventual restoration is the prevention of despair.

CHAPTER II

Satan and Hell

As Milton was writing an epic poem, he needed to have an epic hero. But when we look for the hero in *Paradise Lost*, we come immediately to one of the earliest critical problems about the poem; who *is* the hero? John Dryden remarked in 1697 that *Paradise Lost* was not a satisfactory epic. It would have been truer to its *genre*,

if the Devil had not been his hero instead of Adam; if the giant had not foiled the knight, and driven him out of his stronghold, to wander through the world with his lady errant.[1]

Dryden suggests that though Milton intended Adam as his hero, Adam could not fulfil this role because instead of defeating the traditional giant, he is himself defeated and driven out of his stronghold. The Devil performs the successful exploits fit for an epic hero. Joseph Addison denied 'Mr Dryden's reflection, that the devil was in reality Milton's hero' in *The Spectator*, No. 297:

Paradise Lost is an epic, or a narrative poem, and he that looks for an hero in it, searches for that which Milton never intended; but if he will needs fix the name of an hero upon any person in it, it is certainly the Messiah who is the hero, both in the principal action, and in the chief episodes.[2]

The possibilities for the hero-figure, then, are various. It could be Adam (as Blackmore first suggested), Satan, or Christ; or it could be argued that in this poem there are no heroes. Pagan epic needed a hero because, as Addison went on to say,

Paganism could not furnish out a real action for a fable greater than that of the *Iliad* or *Aeneid*, and therefore an heathen could not form a higher notion of a poem than one of that kind which they call heroic.

If Milton is superseding pagan epic, perhaps he is dispensing with a hero for his Christian epic. Alternatively, perhaps he is superseding

1. John Dryden (ed. W. P. Ker, 1900), *Works*, II.165.
2. Joseph Addison, *The Spectator*, No. 297.

it by having more heroes than a pagan epic—having a trinity of man (Adam), man as fully fallen (Satan) and God as man (Christ) —so representing the full potentialities of man's behaviour from the degradation of Satan to the self-sacrifice and martyrdom of Christ.

The discussion is not merely trivial and should not be dismissed (as Waldock dismisses it) as 'a technical problem'; it is a problem basic to Milton's conception of *Paradise Lost* and the point is not that 'each of the four or five possible answers was equally right— or wrong—since each was the answer to a separate question'[3] but that we should be concerned by the question. We are *meant* to ask who is the hero, to puzzle over what heroism means, to puzzle over the nature of true heroism, and to consider what being fallen means. Because if we decide that Satan is the hero, he is a hero who is fallen, and the values of heroism that he represents ought to be examined with his fall in mind. Does heroism necessarily involve sinfulness?

Satan is in the position of the hero not only in regard to the plot, as Dryden saw, but he is also described and presented in heroic terms. He is the typical epic hero fighting against great odds, refusing to give in. He shares the bravery and defiance of the heroes we so admire in the *Battle of Maldon*, the *Chanson de Roland*, or the story of the Alamo.

> What though the field be lost?
> All is not lost; th'unconquerable Will,
> And study of revenge, immortal hate,
> And courage never to submit or yield:
> And what is else not to be overcome?
> That Glory never shall his wrauth or might
> Extort from me. To bow and sue for grace
> With suppliant knee, and deifie his power
> Who from the terror of this Arm so late
> Doubted his Empire, that were low indeed,
> That were an ignominy and shame beneath
> This downfall; . . .
>
> (I.105-116)

This is Satan's first speech in the poem, and by it he puts himself in this grand heroic tradition—the 'courage never to submit or yield'. It is almost a classic text for the 'we will not give in' theme. Even if the battle, 'the field', be lost, 'All is not lost; th'unconquerable Will' remains. The sonorous, rolling emphatic 'All' sets the tone of the immensities of noble heroism, leading on to the declaration of the refusal to surrender—'th'unconquerable Will'. It is a fine cry of defiance, but it leads directly on to the 'study of revenge'.

3. A. J. A. Waldock, *Paradise Lost and Its Critics* (1947), p. 1.

Even if we find this sentiment only ambiguous—the revenge *may* be justified, like Hamlet's—the next phrase places it in its context: 'immortal hate'. We are not allowed to forget that it is Satan speaking. With the next line, certainly, we return to the noble, heroic defiance—'courage never to submit or yield'—but sandwiched between those two resonant noble cries is the ignoble 'immortal hate', the inglorious '*study* of revenge'.

There are two ways of looking at what is happening here. Satan may be using the traditionally heroic rousing cries, and interweaving his own corrupt sentiments amongst them. It would be a typically Satanic thing to do. Alternatively, since the defiance slips so naturally into the cruelly vengeful hatred, there is the suggestion that heroic gestures of fortitude are of the same order as such ignobility. There is no real contrast or clash—heroism is a cruel and corrupt concept.

As we read carefully the incidents and images that put Satan in the ranks of the traditional heroes, we see how at the same time they are insisting on his corruption. Certainly Satan *is* heroic—but we must not be deluded by ascribing a simple moral worth to his heroism. There is a continual ambiguity. Milton is not undercutting or ridiculing Satan—the intention is less crude than that—but rather preserving an ambiguous balance between what we think of as the noble heroic, and the obviously depraved. The suggestion is that the two are inseparable.

Satan's heroic associations can be seen in the passage describing his leaving the burning lake for the shore in Hell. Milton uses the traditionally sustained epic simile, but not in any digressive way. Eliot referred to 'a kind of inspired *frivolity*' in the details of the simile—not realizing the significance of each aspect for our evaluation of Satan's heroism:

> his ponderous shield
> Ethereal temper, massy, large and round,
> Behind him cast; the broad circumference
> Hung on his shoulders like the Moon, whose Orb
> Through Optic Glass the *Tuscan* Artist views
> At Ev'ning from the top of *Fesole*,
> Or in *Valdarno*, to descry new Lands,
> Rivers or Mountains in her spotty Globe.
> His Spear, to equal which the tallest Pine
> Hewn on *Norwegian* hills, to be the Mast
> Of som great Ammiral, were but a wand,
> He walkd with to support uneasie steps
>
> (I.284-295)

With his shield, Satan is placed with Goliath and Achilles as epic heroes (Biblical and classical), and yet greater even than them.

The pine tree used as a walking stick derives from the description of Polyphemus in the *Aeneid*, and the comparison of Polyphemus' club to a ship's mast comes from the *Odyssey*. Milton has deliberately put himself into a poetical tradition of the epic heroic here by the implicit allusions not only to Homer and Virgil, but to the Renaissance writers Tasso, Ariosto, Sylvester and Cowley.[4] His allusions show that he is writing in a specific tradition, and at the same time they place Satan in a traditional heroic stance.

When we recognize the allusions, though, we realize not merely that Satan is a typical epic hero, but that he is like Polyphemus, the cruel ogre. The description of the spear both puts Satan in a classical heroic tradition, and makes a moral comment on him. Similarly the comparison of the shield to the moon does more than make Satan seem an even greater hero than his literary predecessors because his shield is so much bigger than theirs. In the medieval cosmology that was still part of the seventeenth-century world picture, the moon controlled the sphere of the universe closest to the Earth, a sphere of transitory, changeful things, a sphere subject to chance. It is the sphere that man inhabits—and that appropriately Satan now belongs to; his heavenly stable glory is changing, fading: the moon is an ironically appropriate image. And there is a further appropriateness of the moon to Satan, since his remaining glory as a fallen archangel is merely 'what permissive glory since his fall / Was left him' (X.451)—just as the moon shines only by 'borrowing her Light' from the sun (VII.377). Satan's glory is 'permissive', dependent on what God still allows, just as the moon is dependent on the sun. Moreover, the moon is the illumination of night, and night and darkness are the pervasive image and setting for Hell and sinfulness. An additional richness to the passage is the further complexity of what the telescope reveals. The human reader needs a telescope to have some idea of the size of the moon— and here of the size of Satan, to be able to view him in Hell before he approaches Earth; it is the only way of covering those vast distances and understanding the huge size of the universe, through which Satan moves with ease. Although the telescope reminds us of the size and grandeur and distances of the events, it reveals too the spots on the moon. Satan's shield is, appropriate to his fallen condition, his fading glory, spotty, and spots are marks of evil (V.119). Satan's accoutrements are heroic, but simultaneously marks of his corruption and degradation.

Milton establishes the ambiguous nature of Satan not merely in

4. *See* Davis P. Harding, *The Club of Hercules: studies in the classical background of Paradise Lost* (1962), p. 63 *and* B. Rajan, *Paradise Lost and the Seventeenth Century Reader* (1947), p. 122.

individual instances, but by a sustained pattern of imagery of ennoblement and reduction, of amplification and meiosis, relating separate episodes and descriptions into an interlocking coherent structure. We can see this in the description of Satan rallying his troops like a typical heroic commander:

> he above the rest
> In shape and gesture proudly eminent
> Stood like a Towr; his form had yet not lost
> All her Original brightness, nor appear'd
> Less than Arch-Angel ruind, and th'excess
> Of Glory obscur'd: As when the Sun new ris'n
> Looks through the Horizontal misty Air
> Shorn of his Beams, or from behind the Moon
> In dim Eclipse disastrous twilight sheds
> On half the Nations, and with fear of change
> Perplexes Monarchs. Darkend so, yet shon
> Above them all th' Arch-Angel: but his face
> Deep scars of Thunder had intrencht, . . .
>
> (I.589-601)

The nobility of Satan is insisted on. His role as traditional hero is established once again by allusion to classical literature, the first lines echoing a description of Turnus (*Aeneid* VII.783-4[5]). We are assured too of the angelic; he is called 'Arch-Angel'—'ruind' in line 593, but with no reducing adjective in line 600. He is ennobled, too, by comparison with the sun—its only appearance in the darkened world of Hell—and implicitly with Samson.

But even as he is being ennobled, the process of reduction begins; it is a Samson 'Shorn of his Beams' that the sun is like; it shines through air that is misty, the suggestion of moral confusion we find again when Satan enters Paradise in a mist (IX.180). The equivocal nature of the ennoblement is emphasized by the moon's eclipsing the sun. Similarly, the scars of thunder provoke an equivocal response; they finely suggest Satan's military courage and heroic bravery—'intrencht' is brilliantly appropriate with its reminder of the battlefield. But at the same time the scars are a defacement, marks of his fading glory, scars of defeat like the spots of corruption on his shield, and insignia of his evil in having waged war against God.

The detail of the scars is not only a part of the physical description of Satan; it is part of the sustained imaging of his moral nature, picking up the earlier image of the spotty shield and looking forward to the devilish facial contortions he makes when disguised as a cherub (IV.114-130). The related sun-moon images offer a similar

5. Cf. Harding, *The Club of Hercules*, p. 45.

sustained imaging of Satan's moral nature. Satan's glory has been compared to the sun, but equivocally since it is eclipsed by the moon and dimmed by mist; earlier we saw his huge shield compared to the moon, yet to a spotty moon. Later in his voyage to the Earth, Satan lands on the sun:

> There lands the Fiend, a spot like which perhaps
> Astronomer in the Suns lucent Orbe
> Through his glaz'd Optic Tube yet never saw.
>
> (III.588-590)

The recurrence of the telescope invites a comparison with the spotty moon (I.284). Satan has progressed from holding a spotty moon to being the sun, from being the sun eclipsed to being a sun spot. It is impossible to say which is the better, impossible to see any steady degeneration. Instead, the group of images suggests a consistent equivocalness—the ambiguity of an 'Arch-Angel ruind'.

The process by which Satan is presented is a more ordered and structured one than referring merely to equivocalness or ambiguity might suggest. The terms of the ambiguity are those of the specific pattern of amplification and meiosis—of ennobling and belittling. It is this pattern that controls the presentation of Satan, rather than any rigidly conceived decline. B. Rajan in his argument for the steady degeneration of Satan claims that:

In the fifth book we revert to a Satan who, chronologically, ought to be at his noblest. Instead, we find only a professional politician, a propagandist ... It is a Satan notably different from the Archangel of the first two books.[6]

As Rajan admits, this raises problems about Milton's handling of the character of Satan, that can be answered only by saying he changed his mind, or that he wanted, as Rajan puts it, 'to suggest Satan's tawdriness and triviality when he is measured against the values of Heaven'.[7] It is difficult to avoid making Milton seem too much of an artistic opportunist with that explanation—as if he is careless about the consistency of his story in trying for other effects.

In fact, when we see Satan in Heaven he is not inferior to the Satan in Hell; he is not markedly superior, either. He is still presented by this two-fold pattern. His heavenly glory is insisted upon by the description of his troops:

> Innumerable as the Starrs of Night,
> Or Starrs of Morning, Dew-drops, which the Sun
> Impearls on every leaf and every flower.
>
> (V.745-747)

6. Rajan, *Paradise Lost and the Seventeenth Century Reader*, pp. 101-2.
7. *Paradise Lost and the Seventeenth Century Reader*, p. 102.

It is a beauty that makes nonsense of the statement that he is nobler in Hell than in Heaven; but it is a beauty that is qualified within ten lines by the gaudy splendour of Satan's throne, looking forward to the throne in Hell—

> High on a Hill, far blazing, as a Mount
> Rais'd on a Mount, with Pyramids and Towrs
> From Diamond Quarries hewn and Rocks of Gold,
>
> (V.757-759)

Similarly, Satan's heroic glory is attested in his encounter with Michael when 'two broad Suns thir Shields / Blaz'd opposite' (VI.305-306). Satan's shield is here glorious in contrast with the spotty moon it becomes in Hell; seeing him in this flashback we see his original glory. Yet even here the glory is qualified; it must be put against the ignobility of the war he has created, the destruction he is involved in.

Satan is not less noble in Heaven, but presented consistently by this pattern of amplification and meiosis; and his noble characteristics in Heaven balance the ignoble ones we have already seen. From being discovered like a toad in Paradise, and leaving 'murmuring' in Book IV, he reappears in Heaven as one of the first of the angels. The juxtaposition of his attributes in Hell, Paradise and Heaven, a juxtaposition aided by the distortion of the chronology of the events—complements the ambiguity of the individual images in suggesting his equivocal nature. Certainly there is an overall decline: but the process is neither one of steady descent (for Satan shows traits of nobility right to the end), nor one originating from initial pure glory (for even in Heaven Satan's qualities have been shown as ambiguous).

By not recognizing this pattern of ambiguity, Waldock presented his case of 'the technique of degradation'. He argued that the term degeneration applied to the downward course of Satan had no validity; 'the charges do not generate themselves from within . . . they are imposed from without. Satan . . . does not degenerate: *he is degraded*'.[8] His case was that Milton continually presented Satan too attractively, and so had to degrade his character to conform with the theological scheme. Waldock objected to the lines after Satan's first speech,

> So spake th' Apostat Angel, though in pain,
> Vaunting aloud, but rackt with deep despair:
>
> (I.125-126)

8. *Paradise Lost and Its Critics*, p. 83.

Has there been much despair in what we have just been listening to? The speech would almost seem to be incompatible with that . . . Surely the truth is obvious that the phrase is half mechanical: it is the first of a long line of automatic snubs, of perfunctory jabs and growls. Each great speech lifts Satan a little beyond what Milton really intended, so he suppresses him again (or tries to) in a comment.[9]

Yet the speech does show some despair in its broken opening line of grief—'If thou beest he; But O how fall'n.' The rest of it, though, cannot show despair because Satan has to present a proud and courageous front. Milton is not snubbing Satan but showing how greatly he suffers and how greatly he must dissimulate. As leader he must vaunt aloud—but he realizes the misery of the situation. The conclusion serves as a balance to the speech: the glory and defiance proclaimed are qualified by the inner despair and defeat that cannot be revealed to his followers. Satan is given a dramatic freedom for ennoblement that is balanced by the narrative framework of reduction. The two together form a haunting chord.

Milton is not accidentally creating a Satan too noble, and then having to discredit him. He is creating a fully ambiguous Satan, a character both noble and debased, who is described from the beginning by simultaneous images of amplification and meiosis. Certainly in the course of the poem he becomes more debased; but the seeds of degradation were presented in the basic ambiguity from the beginning, not, as Waldock would argue, superimposed.

Part of the success of the character of Satan is that he develops. The devils in the debate in Hell are brilliantly presented figures; Milton has made them general yet individual, and they could so easily have slipped into humours or caricature. He avoids that danger successfully. They are still presented, though, as static figures; they are not involved in any action, their characters do not develop or unfold. Nor do the characters of the angels—Raphael, Gabriel, and Michael. But Satan, Adam and Eve are presented as characters in action; their behaviour alters, their attitudes change.

The heroic schemes in Hell have a certain grandeur about them. Attempting to regain the lost Heaven is a creative plan; the devils parody God's creation grotesquely—but at least Pandæmonium is something created. By the time Satan reaches Earth, however, even this perverted nobility is fading, and he no longer considers creating anything. The hope of regaining Heaven that he still had in Hell (II.397) has been replaced by the plan of merely spiting God with the destruction of man. The creation of gunpowder in

9. *Paradise Lost and Its Critics*, pp. 78-9.

Heaven, the building of Pandæmonium in Hell, have finally—
and perhaps predictably—given way to mere destruction—

> For onely in destroying I find ease
> To my relentless thoughts; . . .

(IX.129-130)

The development of Satan's character is also a degradation. That is made tragically clear when Ithuriel and Zephon discover him in Paradise, yet fail to recognize him:

> Know ye not then said *Satan*, filld with scorn,
> Know ye not mee? . . .

(IV.827-828)

And they do not know him. All they know from his appearance is that he is a fallen angel. As Zephon says,

> Think not, revolted Spirit, thy shape the same,
> Or undiminisht brightness, to be known
> As when thou stoodst in Heav'n upright and pure;
> That Glorie then, when thou no more wast good,
> Departed from thee, and thou resembl'st now
> Thy sin and place of doom obscure and foul.

(IV.835-840)

Satan's glory is fading. He thinks it is merely 'outward lustre' (I.97), but in the universe of *Paradise Lost* outward appearance is a mark of the character's moral state. Satan's moral degeneration is demonstrated; he begins to look like Hell. The epic hero of Book I, declaiming vengeance and defiance, becomes the disguised liar who destroys the woman, not even the man. Adam and Eve are misguided in expecting Satan chivalrously to attack the man first (IX.305, 382). Eve does not 'much expect / A Foe so proud will first the weaker seek'—but Satan's heroic pride has now waned.

Even in this degradation, however, Satan is still a figure to be reckoned with. C. S. Lewis claimed that 'mere Christianity commits every Christian to believing that "the Devil is (in the long run) an ass".'[10] But Milton does not make his Satan an ass; he is never presented as contemptible. Morally contemptible he certainly becomes: but he does, like Hamlet, succeed in his revenge. Hamlet produces his own death, Satan heaps worse suffering on his own head—but each succeeds. Certainly God will produce man's redemption—but that does not minimize the effectiveness of the havoc Satan has produced—and Milton nowhere minimizes Satan's success in that.

10. C. S. Lewis, *A Preface to Paradise Lost* (1942), p. 93.

And Satan never becomes *totally* degraded. Had he done so, he would have been uninteresting—merely a villain steeped in evil. Milton brilliantly lets him retain some 'good' feelings—so that he is always conscious of the evil he is doing; he is never evil enough to be unaware. When he comes across Eve alone, for a moment he stands 'Stupidly good, of enmitie disarmd, / Of guile, of hate, of envie, of revenge' (IX.465-466); after the Fall has been achieved, 'Back to the Thicket slunk / The guiltie Serpent' (IX.784-785). For all his declamations of 'Evil be thou my good' Satan remains aware of what good is; he destroys by a compulsion and always knows he is doing evil. There is a tension between his instinctive feelings and his compulsion, between his residual moral sense and his avowed aims—a tension that aggravates his Hell, and that makes him a 'conscious' villain, a fascinating character not a mere first murderer.

Of course not every manifestation of Satan's heroism is accompanied by a countering reminder of his corruption. His defiance can be splendid—as, for instance, when he is detected by the angels in Paradise. He is surrounded by celestial troops, yet not at all cowed. When Gabriel asks him why he left Hell, he summons up a biting sarcasm in these fully dramatic lines:

> *Gabriel,* thou hadst in Heav'n th' esteem of wise,
> And such I held thee; but this question askt
> Puts me in doubt. Lives there who loves his pain?
>
> (IV.886-888)

And when Gabriel tells him to leave, otherwise he will be put in chains, Satan gives a magnificent reply:

> Then when I am thy captive talk of chains,
> Proud limitarie Cherube . . .
>
> (IV.970-971)

It is splendidly heroic. The un-English construction of 'lives there who loves his pain?' does not distress us as uncolloquial because it is so vividly terse. The staccato concision is so appropriate to Satan at this point, and Milton's verse is the superbly flexible medium that can create it, as well as create the rhetorical declamations of Satan addressing his followers in Hell. There he needed the rolling periods, the polysyllablism; here, in a tough corner, he is the tight-lipped, defiant soldier. He will open up enough to be contemptuous of his enemies. He answers questions, but he will give nothing away:

23

thus much what was askt.
The rest is true, they found me where they say;
But that implies not violence or harm.

(IV.899-901)

The heroic is not qualified here, because it has been qualified so often. The Devil is given his due. He is allowed to be unequivocally heroic because by this stage we have read enough to make us doubtful of any heroic values. His heroism, his bravery here, after all, are used for something ultimately so unheroic. In a small, limited view such as we are given in this close-up of Satan's encounter with the angelic troops, he seems to be brave; in a fuller and wider context, in a larger view, his bravery and heroism are seen in a different light. When God looks from Heaven (III.56-76) his panoramic vision includes a sight of Satan ending his courageous lone voyage; but includes, too, a sight of the innocent Adam and Eve Satan is journeying to destroy. The bravery of Satan's epic journey is put in the larger moral context of its ignoble, destructive purpose.

Bravery, courage, defiance are too easily misapplied and used for immoral or ignoble purposes. This realization lies at the basis of Milton's repudiation of the heroic in *Paradise Lost*. And he does repudiate it, not only by showing the ambiguous moral nature of heroism, but by an explicit rejection. Satan is implicitly compared to Achilles, Ulysses and Aeneas; the devils are described in a simile putting them in the same category as (but far superior to) other heroic figures of epic, fable and romance (I.573-587). Not only are Satan and the devils shown in conventional heroic actions and events, or described by traditional heroic similes, they are associated with named literary figures of heroism. All this is called to mind in the invocation to Book IX, where Milton gives his great repudiation of heroic poetry, and heroic values. Satan has been allowed to run his heroic course, and we have seen what that is leading to: in Book IX he will corrupt Adam and Eve. The heroic has been allowed to damn itself. Milton now explicitly disavows it, to offer the Christian values of 'Patience and Heroic Martyrdom'. They are the theme of the remaining books of the poem. Satan, the traditional hero, is about to achieve success, and Milton will now leave the classic heroic to present the tragedy of the Fall— and the Christian values to arise from it.

Sad task, yet argument
Not less but more Heroic than the wrauth
Of stern *Achilles* on his Foe persu'd
Thrice Fugitive about *Troy* Wall; or rage

24

> Of *Turnus* for *Lavinia* disespous'd,
> Or *Neptunes* ire or *Juno*'s, that so long
> Perplexd the *Greek* and *Cytherea*'s Son; . . . .
>
> Not sedulous by Nature to indite
> Warrs, hitherto the onely Argument
> Heroic deemd, chief maistrie to dissect
> With long and tedious havoc fabl'd Knights
> In Battels feignd; the better fortitude
> Of Patience and Heroic Martyrdom
> Unsung; . . .

$$\text{(IX.13-19, 27-33)}$$

The question of who is the hero and what is heroism can now be seen in its full importance. Satan may have had heroic qualities, the devils may have been braver than any recorded heroes, but such heroism and bravery are destructive. Milton makes this even more explicit when he deals with the 'Giants' on Earth in the vision of the future shown to Adam.

> Such were these Giants, men of high renown;
> For in those dayes Might onely shall be admir'd,
> And Valour and Heroic Vertue calld;
> To overcome in Battel, and subdue
> Nations, and bring home spoils with infinite
> Man-slaughter, shall be held the highest pitch
> Of human Glorie, and for Glorie done
> Of triumph, to be styl'd great Conquerors,
> Patrons of Mankind, Gods, and Sons of Gods,
> Destroyers rightlier calld and Plagues of men.
> Thus Fame shall be achiev'd, renown on Earth,
> And what most merits fame in silence hid.

$$\text{(XI.688-699)}$$

The record of the 'Giants' in *Genesis* (VI.4) was very brief, and hardly necessitated the treatment Milton gave to it. But his comments apply (as Harding has pointed out[11]) fittingly to the code of the Homeric heroes—and to Satan; 'Destroyers rightlier calld and Plagues of men' reminds us that 'The Destroyer' was one of the names of Satan, and that the fallen angels had been compared to the plague of locusts in Egypt (I.338-343). Satan and the fallen angels represent a military heroism. The war in Heaven, Satan tells Michael, is:

> The strife which thou callst evil, but wee style
> The strife of Glorie: . . .

$$\text{(VI.289-290)}$$

11. *The Club of Hercules*, pp. 42-3.

For someone who had lived through the Civil War, military glory might not seem one of man's proud achievements. Through the march of General Monk's army on London the Protectorate came to an end and Charles II was restored. Military heroism, military bravery, was something that could be applied to ignoble ends too readily.

Although Milton is repudiating the worth of the old Homeric code and offering heroic martyrdom as a better courage, he is still using the traditional heroic concepts for their literary effect on us. We admire Satan because of the colouring he has from similes applied to Achilles, Aeneas and Turnus, because of his bravery in heroic encounters. We are always conscious of his evil, cruelty and fallen state—and it is appropriate for Milton's repudiation of the heroic that his hero should be dishonest, evil and cruel: such is (or at least can be) heroism. Satan's subtle wiles remind us of Ulysses (to whom he is compared in passing, II.1019)—but the ennoblement from that comparison only balances the unadmirable slyness of the deceptions: and that, of course, reflects back on to Ulysses.

To see that Satan is in the position of epic hero in *Paradise Lost*, and to see that he is compared to other epic heroes, is not at all the same thing as saying that he is the ideal hero, the figure we should admire. But by being the epic hero, he has slipped into this other position. 'The reason Milton wrote in fetters when he wrote of Angels and God, and at liberty when of Devils and Hell, is because he was a true Poet and of the Devil's party without knowing it', William Blake wrote in *The Marriage of Heaven and Hell* in 1793. Shelley, in *A Defence of Poetry* (1821), wrote similarly, claiming it as 'the most decisive proof of the supremacy of Milton's genius' that Satan is presented as the hero whom we admire:

Nothing can exceed the energy and magnificence of the character of Satan as expressed in *Paradise Lost*. It is a mistake to suppose that he could ever have been intended for the popular personification of evil . . . Milton's Devil as a moral being is as far superior to his God, as one who perseveres in some purpose which he has conceived to be excellent in spite of adversity and torture, is to one who in the cold security of undoubted triumph inflicts the most horrible revenge upon his enemy, not from any mistaken notion of inducing him to repent of a perseverance in enmity, but with the alleged design of exasperating him to new torments.[12]

But objections to the cruelty of Milton's God do not make Satan an admirable figure. Certainly Satan must have some motives for

12. P. B. Shelley, *Works* (1880), VII, pp. 127-8.

his actions, some seeming provocation; certainly he must be in some way appealing (as are his arguments to Eve)—else how could he be so effective in the world? But the Romantic view of Satan as ideal hero is too simple. Helen Gardner has argued that Satan shares some typical features of the tragic heroes like Faustus and Macbeth; like them he has an 'incapacity for change to a better state'; like them he is presented through soliloquies.[13] Yet Milton seems to be trying to do something far more difficult than present Satan as a Romantic or tragic hero: he is trying for an effect of increasing alienation. Satan is presented at first as someone who is still noble, still brave, still proud, still has some angelic virtue left; but as his glory fades and he sinks deeper into evil, the reader draws further and further from him. It is an alienation effect depending partly on the fact of our withdrawal from the values of the old heroic code, partly on the increasing degradation of Satan. With the tragic hero we watch in fascinated horror as he plunges himself into greater corruption; with Satan, the effect is different. We see him first, as Shelley did, with sympathy. But at the end he is immensely distanced from us, reduced to a serpent in the depths of Hell—distanced geographically, emotionally and morally. The personal tragedy of Satan—so powerful in his soliloquies of Book IV—has been replaced by the personal tragedy of Eve, and the huge archangel has been reduced to the slinking snake who no longer has emotions that concern us.

Much of our sympathy for Satan is of the sort we feel for the tragic hero—the sense of waste, of so much potential so misused, so corrupted. This carries with it, nevertheless, a moral commentary —the potential *corrupted*. But Milton has also created a sympathy for Satan from his loss, his exclusion from happiness, his being perpetually an outsider, and our sympathy can persist here whatever morally we think of Satan; whether we feel with Shelley that he is admirable, or whether we feel that he is wholly evil, we can still respond to this image of exclusion and exile.

His loneliness is one of the results of his pride, in refusing to allow equals or rivals, and of his position as a leader with responsibility that he cannot delegate. He makes the journey to Earth alone, cutting short the debate so that no one else will be able to offer and win admiration. His journey, however, represents more than merely his enacted pride. It becomes an image of his solitariness and isolation; when he visits the place later to be known as the Paradise of Fools his loneliness there becomes an image of his fate.

13. Helen Gardner, *A Reading of Paradise Lost* (1965), p. 99ff.

> So on this windie Sea of Land, the Fiend
> Walkd up and down alone bent on his prey,
> Alone, for other Creature in this place
> Living or liveless to be found was none,
>
> (III.440-443)

This passage with its plangent repetition of 'alone', re-emphasized at the beginning of a line, and its dwelling on the lack of life— 'none' echoing as a visual rhyme 'alone'—does not merely show that the Paradise of Fools is not yet opened. Why go to pains to make that point, after all? It demonstrates the loneliness of Satan's voyage, of Satan's whole wandering life now. Rather different is the state of Adam and Eve at the end of the poem when

> They hand in hand with wandring steps and slow,
> Through *Eden* took thir solitarie way.
>
> (XII.648-649)

At first there might seem to be a parallel with Satan when he 'Explores his solitary flight' (II.632); but the solitariness of Adam and Eve is a solitariness that is not solitary, that is shared with each other, that is supported by the company of each other, and that has, moreover, 'Providence thir guide' (XII.647). Satan is totally alone, unguided—and wretched. As Adam says to God before Eve has been created,

> In solitude
> What happiness, who can enjoy alone,
> Or all enjoying, what contentment find?
>
> (VIII.364-366)

God of course is alone, as he points out to Adam (VIII.399ff.)— but it is a singleness of perfection. Satan's loneliness is an ironic parody of God's. It is a loneliness of exclusion, of deprivation, of exile. When he sees Adam and Eve together, their happiness serves only to emphasize his own solitude, and he

> to himself thus plaind.
> Sight hateful, sight tormenting! thus these two
> Imparadis't in one anothers arms
> The happier *Eden*, shall enjoy thir fill
> Of bliss on bliss, while I to Hell am thrust,
> Where neither joy nor love, but fierce desire,
> Among our other torments not the least,
> Still unfulfilld with pain of longing pines;
>
> (IV.504-511)

The endless suffering is caught with the word-play of pain and pines picking up 'plaind', and the dragging movement of the last two

28

lines, broken by no caesura. And the happiness of Adam and Eve—
'thir fill / Of bliss on bliss'—contrasts not only with Satan's desire
'still unfulfilld', rhyme and alliteration enforcing the contrast, but
also with his earlier description of his own endless suffering:

> And in the lowest deep a lower deep
> Still threatening to devour me opens wide,
>
> (IV.76-77)

The bliss of Adam and Eve is a building up, bliss *on* bliss; Satan's
suffering is an endless fall, a continual decline. Perhaps it is because
of his suffering that it is Satan who gives the haunting description
of Adam and Eve's happiness—'Imparadis't in one anothers arms'.

Satan's exclusion was unforgettably imaged on his voyage to
Eden when he passed the stairs leading to Heaven.

> The Stairs were then let down, whether to dare
> The Fiend by easie ascent, or aggravate
> His sad exclusion from the dores of Bliss.
>
> (III.523-525)

We may dislike the idea of God the joker taunting Satan with the
dangling stairs, but it is more than compensated for by that fine
evocation of perpetual exile. It is this loss that arouses our sympathy
for Satan. It arouses our sympathy because it is, after all, a theme
basic to the poem—to Paradise *Lost*. The same sadness of Satan's
loss and exile is present with Adam and Eve later, notably in their
expulsion from Paradise. The difference is that Adam and Eve
have the hope of salvation and restoration. Satan does not; he is
doomed to perpetual isolation. It is this that has made him so
appealing a Romantic and Existentialist figure.

The pattern of amplification-meiosis, of juxtaposed images of
ennoblement and reduction that capture Satan's ambiguity, was a
pattern consistently used in seventeenth-century religious poetry.
Rosemond Tuve has described its nature and its application in her
Elizabethan and Metaphysical Imagery:

In Herbert, who shows chiefly just those elements of mysticism which in
some degree pervade all Christian devotional poetry, the juxtaposition of
meiosis and amplification generally results from the paradox of man's
insignificance and his greatness as child and heir of God. Man's worth is
amplified with 'The starres have us to bed', or with the old image of 'Man
is one world, and hath / Another to attend him.' Seemingly diminished by
'He is a tree,' 'A beast', his worth is as quickly amplified by the immediate
addition of 'yet bears more fruit', 'yet is, or should be more'. . . . He can
be haled with a metaphor from the mean to the transcendent and back

again within the frame of a single short poem, without the slightest offense to decorum; this contrast is part of Herbert's subject, and his images properly obey it.[14]

The contrast is part of Milton's subject similarly. Satan as one of the first of the angels, as a figure of such potential, became the enemy of God. He is appropriately described in this pattern. But he is described in it, too, because he is an image of fallen man in *Paradise Lost*; fallen man's similarity to Satan and the other fallen angels is emphasized by this established rhetorical pattern. Man has the potential for nobleness, bravery, courage and activity that Satan has; but it is allied, as with Satan, with a potential for degradation, evil, cruelty. The downward career of fallen mankind is seen in that of Satan.

The hero of the epic poem was traditionally a character to be admired, a figure on whom to model human behaviour. It is a terrible irony that Satan is in the position of the hero of *Paradise Lost*; Satan, for fallen man, is indeed the model of behaviour. This hero is not someone who ought to be, but someone who regrettably is, admired. The implications of Milton's chosen poetical form make a tragic irony.

It is not just that man's evil is modelled on Satan. Milton shows in Satan and the devils the activities, thoughts, behaviour, even virtues, of fallen man. As Goethe remarked, 'What one admires in Milton's Satan, is the human'.[15]

Apart from the ironic function, this was necessary to establish the interest of the poem. One of the difficulties of Milton's theme was that since Adam and Eve were innocent they could not show most of the characteristics of mankind. So Milton presents those characteristics in a character already fallen—Satan. The poem had to begin with Satan not just because of the epic tradition of starting in the middle of the action, but because Satan is the only character who can provide sufficient human interest until Adam and Eve are fallen, or at least until their fall is being actively prepared.

Milton used Satan and Hell to fulfil another of the demands of epic—the vision or prediction of the future. Certainly the last two books provide a vision—but it is one of the Biblical 'future'. Satan and Hell present the future of humanity as it will be in the modern world; the future for Adam in the seventeenth-century contemporary world of Milton's readers. So the cosmic drama of good and evil is related to the particular historical time, giving an immediacy

14. Rosemond Tuve, *Elizabethan and Metaphysical Imagery* (Chicago, 1947), p. 225.
15. Goethe, *Weimarer Ausgabe*, I.xi.211.

and relevance for its readers. With Satan and Hell we are shown the technology, trade, discovery, intellectual debate, heroism of fallen man. Adam cannot show this—he presents man's innocence, and after the Fall man's potential for 'patience and heroic martyrdom'. Satan and his fellows in their actions and in the similes by which they are described, show the specific responses of humanity to the Fall; that is why, as Martz points out,[16] so much of the imagery in Hell is geographically specific. The proper names are there to insist that what we see in Hell is like what is going on in the world here and now, or that has gone on in the revolutions of history.

So Satan becomes an image of fallen man, Hell an image of the fallen world, of the earthly city. Louis Martz quotes from St Augustine:

And so the two cities have been fashioned by two loves, the earthly city by the love of self to the contempt of God, the heavenly city by the love of God to the contempt of self.[17]

The egoism, the pride, the 'love of self to the contempt of God' are shown clearly by the fallen angels; Hell is the earthly city in that sense. But Hell is also a city because one of the consequences of the Fall of man was organized social life. Men were originally created free, Milton argues in his *Tenure of Kings and Magistrates* and

they lived so, till from the root of Adam's transgression falling among themselves to do wrong and violence, and foreseeing that such courses must needs tend to the destruction of them all, they agreed by common league to bind each other from mutual injury, and jointly to defend themselves against any that gave disturbance or opposition to such agreement. Hence came cities, towns, and commonwealths.[18]

Eden is a place of rural innocence, an idyllic pastoral world of freedom. But Hell is a fallen world and an image of the organized urban social world of fallen man—and Hell is the reason, too, why such a world developed. When Satan examines Paradise he is described 'As one who long in populous City pent, / Where Houses thick and Sewers annoy the Air' (IX.445-446) is now out in the country, taking the air in the rural innocence of Eden. Afterwards, when he has achieved his mission, he returns to '*Pandæmonium*, Citie and proud seat / Of Lucifer'. (X.424-425).

Cities and Commonwealths resulting from the Fall necessitated political organization, hence the political debate in Hell, and the political imagery in which the immediate results of the Fall are

16. Louis L. Martz, *The Paradise Within* (1964), p. 112.
17. *The Paradise Within*, p. 116.
18. Burton, p. 191.

described (IX.1125ff.). But as Milton argued in his *Tenure*, cities and Commonwealths were produced because man was fallen, and because man was fallen the chosen leaders fell into corruption: 'the temptation of such power, left absolute in their hands, perverted them at length to injustice and partiality'.[19] Satan is presented as such a corrupt ruler, as a political tyrant. 'Surely it is not for nothing that tyrants, by a kind of natural instinct, both hate and fear none more than the true church and saints of God', Milton wrote.[20] Satan, as the archetypal enemy of God, is the archetypal tyrant, and his tyranny is established by a set of images whose implications would be immediately apparent to the seventeenth-century reader—images of rulers of the Eastern world. He is, indeed, explicitly called tyrannical when he claims in a soliloquy that he does not want to hurt Adam's and Eve's 'harmless innocence', but *has* to: Milton describes his excuse as 'necessitie, / The Tyrants plea'. (IV.393-394).

All the anti-Christian cruelty, all the political tyranny of Eastern rulers (in the seventeenth-century view) is brought into play in the descriptions of the splendour of Satan's throne and realm. Remembering that in *Eikonoklastes* Milton compared Charles I's rule of England to Turkish tyranny, we can appreciate the description of Satan:

> High on a Throne of Royal State, which far
> Outshon the wealth of *Ormus* and of *Ind*,
> Or where the gorgeous East with richest hand
> Showrs on her Kings *Barbaric* Pearl and Gold,
> *Satan* exalted sat, . . .
>
> (II.1-5)

'Royal' may be here (and 'Monarchal pride' at II.428 also) a pejorative word for the Republican Milton; the only true king was God, and earthly kings represented God: Satan certainly did not do that so, like Charles, was evil. '*Barbaric* Pearl' is of course a contrast with Heaven's pearly gates and their 'liquid pearl' (III.519). As Sir Thomas Browne wrote in *Christian Morals*, 'To enjoy true happiness we must travel into a very far Countrey, and even out of our selves; for the Pearl we seek for is not to be found in the Indian, but in the Empyrean Ocean'.[21] '*Barbaric*' evokes a related strain of imagery applied to Satan and the devils. We recall their rising from the burning lake, 'hovering' like locusts,

19. Burton, p. 191.
20. Burton, p. 200.
21. *The Works of Sir Thomas Browne* (ed. G. Keynes, 1964) I.278.

Till, as a signal giv'n, th' uplifted Spear
Of thir great Sultan waving to direct
Thir course, in even ballance down they light
On the firm brimstone, and fill all the Plain;
A multitude, like which the populous North
Pourd never from her frozen loins, to pass
Rhene or the *Danaw*, when her barbarous Sons
Came like a Deluge on the South, and spred
Beneath *Gibraltar* to the *Lybian* sands.

(I.347-355)

The '*Barbaric* Pearl' looks back to this description of the devils as barbarians, just as the idea here of Satan as a 'Sultan' looks forward to his Eastern-style splendid throne. The two sets of imagery are interrelated to suggest the extent of Satan's tyranny, to form complementary impressions. Whereas the East represents a sort of productive wealth, and reminds us of the trading voyages and man's mercantile activities, the barbarians produce nothing. They come from 'frozen loins', they are infertile, unproductive—merely destructive. We shall see the devils as creative—building Pandæmonium for instance; but the comparison with the barbarians reminds us of their great destructiveness, wiping out the achievements of civilization, destroying a whole culture. It is a two-way simile: not only is it appropriate for Satan's destructiveness, but the destructiveness of the barbarians is an example of the Satanic evil acting in mankind—Hell acting on Earth. The recurrent Eastern images represent an organized tyranny, such as Satan has in Hell; while the barbarians represent a destruction of social living, of the societies created to repair the damage of the Fall. Their anarchy complements the oriental tyranny to show the social and political disorder of the fallen world. Readers like Shelley have with good reason found Milton's God tyrannous—but Satan and the devils offer no preferable political system.

The gain of knowledge by the Fall led also to the development of science and technology; and in the fallen world technology became necessary. Eden lost its clement climate and became cold at night, so something had to be invented to produce warmth. Adam discusses ways of making fire (X.1069ff.). In the same way Hell needs technology to make it less hideous, whereas in the unfallen Paradise and in Heaven, there was no need for scientific invention.

The identification of natural science with forbidden knowledge was a medieval notion that persisted into the sixteenth and seventeenth centuries.[22] Appropriately, then, Satan invents gunpowder from 'materials dark and crude' (VI.478) in Heaven. Why such

22. Basil Willey, *The Seventeenth Century Background* (1934), p. 35.

materials should be in Heaven, even if underground, is puzzling—
and worrying for the implications it makes about Milton's God.
The result is the creation of cannon.

> These in thir dark Nativitie the Deep
> Shall yield us pregnant with infernal flame,
> Which into hollow Engins long and round
> Thick-rammd, at th' other bore with touch of fire
> Dilated and infuriat shall send forth
> From far with thundring noise among our foes
> Such implements of mischief . . .
>
> (VI.482-488)

It is one of the many devilish parodies of God's creation that occur
in the poem—and this one is in effect the creation of Hell. These
words, 'dark', 'the Deep', 'infernal flame', 'thundring noise',
'mischief'—all presage the Hell to which the devils will be sent,
the Hell which Satan creates in Heaven first by his cannon, by
his war on God.

It is the first scientific creation, too: in Hell we see the full
development of man's scientific skills. An obvious example of them
is the building of Pandæmonium. John Peter has argued that 'it is
strange that angels as yet unfallen should take all night to cast
their cannon (VI.492-3, 521-2) when after their fall they build the
enormous Pandæmonium in a matter of hours. (I.697)'.[23] It may
seem strange; we are meant to think about it, and to realize that
it is quite natural. By the time the angels have fallen to Hell they
are more skilled in technology so can work faster and, more importantly, they are plunged deeper into evil. Their creations are all of
evil, and the more evil they become, the more proficient they get.
But Pandæmonium is not merely a place of evil. It is a type of all
such palaces on Earth—as the palaces it is compared to suggest—
though far superior. The detailed and specific description insists on
our seeing it in terms of earthly architecture.

> Built like a Temple, where *Pilasters* round
> Were set, and Doric pillars overlaid
> With Golden Architrave; nor did there want
> Cornice or Freeze, with bossy Sculptures grav'n,
> The Roof was fretted Gold. . . .
>
> (I.713-717)

Addison objected strongly to the architectural terms used in this
passage, and to other technical terms used elsewhere by Milton—
terms of seamanship and astronomy and the like.[24] But by using

23. John Peter, *A Critique of Paradise Lost* (1960), p. 76.
24. Addison, *The Spectator*, No. 297.

such obviously technical language Milton is emphasizing the technological results of the Fall; our attention is drawn to Pandæmonium not merely as an object occupying the ground in an interesting, aesthetic way—but as something planned and contrived by architectural *knowledge*—a knowledge that has produced its own jargon. This language of man's is a direct result of the Fall—and it is in Hell that we see it applied.

Most of the Devil's technology is military, and the imagery of gunpowder, cannon and explosions follows Satan as he travels. The technological achievements become converted into images of the state of being fallen. When Ithuriel pricks him with a spear in Paradise, Satan explodes:

> As when a spark
> Lights on a heap of nitrous Powder, laid
> Fit for the Tun som Magazin to store
> Against a rumord Warr, the Smuttie grain
> With sudden blaze diffus'd, inflames the Air:
>
> (IV.814-818)

It is a vivid simile, suitable for the great energy of Satan, suitably destructive and aggressive. Appropriate to the whole imagery of Hell, moreover, it suggests he carries Hell with him.

Gunpowder and firearms have an especial appropriateness for Satan as a recurrent image, since they dramatize what we were told about him early in the poem. God

> Left him at large to his own dark designs,
> That with reiterated crimes he might
> Heap on himself damnation, while he sought
> Evil to others, . . .
>
> (I.213-216)

The idea is that of the engineer hoist with his own petard, the revenger of Jacobean drama destroyed by his own revenges. Satan plays this classic part. The appropriate image for this process, of course, is that of the recoil of the cannon. As he enters the serpent, Satan soliloquizes

> Revenge, at first though sweet,
> Bitter ere long back on it self recoils;
>
> (IX.171-172)

It is an image that already contains its own irony, for it was Satan who invented cannon; since he invented cannon, they are bound to recoil, for all the evil he does recoils. And so, aptly, when touched by Ithuriel's spear, he recoils like his own cannon, explodes like his own invention.

Satan's military heroism is supplemented by a heroism of maritime endeavour, and a sequence of imagery associates him with contemporary and modern traders and discoverers. This is a heroism already celebrated in epic poetry—the Portuguese *Lusiads* (1572) dealt with the voyage of Vasco da Gama—and so Satan is associated with a modern epic hero as well as with classical ones. Satan leaves his oriental world of splendour and is compared to a fleet 'Close sailing from *Bengala*, or the Iles / Of *Ternate* and *Tidore*, whence Merchants bring / Thir spicie Drugs' (II.638-640). His voyage is followed in the imagery: here he is flying toward the Cape, and when he approaches Paradise he is compared 'to them who sail / Beyond the *Cape of Hope*' (IV.159-160) in another sustained simile. The similes of this group are always applied to Satan—both showing his courage as an intrepid sea-traveller, and showing in Satan activities of mankind in the fallen world.

Leaving his Eastern trading-world, Satan it is implied is looking for some primitive people to exploit. The seafaring images chart his voyage until finally, as he approaches Eve, he is compared to

> a Ship by skilful Steersman wrought
> Nigh Rivers mouth or Foreland, where the Wind
> Veers oft, as oft so steers, and shifts her Sail;
>
> (IX.513-515)

At his journey's end Satan is not in a port (as perhaps he had expected, II.1044) because Adam and Eve in their innocence and simplicity have created nothing like the industrial or mercantile world of Hell. Eden is an undeveloped land found for the first time by Satan the explorer-trader. He expects, of course, to find mankind easy to exploit—primitive savages. But the irony is that he sees

> Two of far nobler shape erect and tall,
> Godlike erect, with native Honour clad
> In naked Majestie seemd Lords of all,
>
> (IV.288-290)

They are not 'naked' savages or savage 'natives' inferior to Satan, but possessors of a primitive innocence much superior. Satan's scheme has recoiled.

Yet it recoils again with a further irony; for despite their innocence and 'Majestie', Satan does succeed. And his success is marked by a continuation of this pattern of imagery. After the Fall Adam and Eve look for covering for their nakedness.

> Those Leaves
> They gatherd, broad as *Amazonian* Targe,
> And with what skill they had, together sowd,

> To gird thir waist, vain Covering if to hide
> Thir guilt and dreaded shame; O how unlike
> To that first naked Glorie. Such of late
> *Columbus* found th' *American* so girt
> With featherd Cincture, naked else and wilde
> Among the Trees on Iles and woodie Shores.

(IX.1110-1118)

The images have now come to their logical conclusion. The simile ends the voyage with the 'Iles and woodie Shores' at last reached by a famous explorer, Satan is ashore not in a port, not even in the idyllic pastoral Eden, but amongst primitives; he leaves Adam and Eve the savages that the similes suggested he would find them in 'this new World' (IV.391).

Now that they are fallen, images from the fallen world become fully appropriate. The irony that Satan finds not savages but lordly figures has been superseded by the far more tragic irony that he leaves them like primitive savages. He has fulfilled his role as trader-explorer by trading with Adam and Eve to achieve their downfall. Eve traded her birthright, traded Eden, for a worthless bauble, for the 'fair enticing Fruit' (IX.996) that becomes 'that fallacious Fruit' (IX.1046). The apple is like the traditional trading 'beads and glasses' by whose 'false glitter' merchants 'abuse' 'poor Indians' which Milton refers to in *The Reason of Church Government*.[25] It costs Satan nothing, it is not even his tree. Once again the activities of fallen men are presented through Satan.

The activities of Satan and the devils take on symbolic qualities in the course of *Paradise Lost*. The cannon Satan invents become, with their recoil, a symbol of evil recoiling on itself. Similarly after the devils' philosophic discussions have come to nothing and they have 'found no end, in wandring mazes lost' (II.561), the 'maze' becomes a recurrent image of deception, confusion, and deceit. Significantly, from the beginning it is a two-fold term. The philosophy the devils discuss is a maze that will confuse people, obscure the true faith, and the devils will encourage it in the fallen world. But the devils are themselves lost in the maze of their philosophy, in the labyrinth of their own language as the verse suggests; what is the way out of those packed nouns—'Providence, Foreknowledge, Will, and Fate, / Fixt Fate, free Will, Foreknowledge absolute' (II.559-560)?

Preparing to seduce Eve, Satan looks for the serpent 'in whose mazie folds / To hide me' and discovers it 'In labyrinth of many a round self-roul'd' (IX.161-162, 183); he approaches Eve 'a surging

25. Burton, p. 348 *and* cf. William Empson, *Some Versions of Pastoral* (1935), p. 171.

Maze' (IX.499). The image is so firmly established that Milton can punningly echo it when Eve, hearing the serpent speak, is 'Not unamaz'd' (IX.552).

As an image of deception and confusion, the maze is fully appropriate. But does it imply Satan is a victim of his own mazes, is he lost in his labyrinth like the philosophizing devils? C. S. Lewis claimed that indeed the 'doom of Nonsense' had descended on Satan, and he cited Satan's speech by which he argues that Hell's government will be secure: the leader suffers most from God, so no one will try to unseat the leader to take his place, for there is no one—

> whose portion is so small
> Of present pain, that with ambitious mind
> Will covet more. . . .
>
> (II.33-35)

Hence he concludes that the infernal monarchy has a stability which the celestial lacks. That the obedient angels might love to obey is an idea which cannot cross his mind even as a hypothesis. But even within this invincible ignorance contradiction breaks out; for Satan makes this ludicrous proposition a reason for hoping ultimate victory. He does not, apparently, notice, that every approach to victory must take away the grounds on which victory is hoped.[26]

The trap Lewis fell into here was of taking Satan's speech to be true to Satan's thoughts and beliefs. That was the mistake Eve made, to believe what the serpent said was true. But Satan had never eaten the apple as he claimed: nor need we believe he believes in his argument here. It is a political speech addressed to his followers. The despair in the opening of Book IV shows Satan speaking only for himself, not putting on a show for his fellows. In Book II he uses this false logic not because he is deceived, but in order to deceive his followers—to raise their hopes, and to discourage them from rivalling his claim to leadership. The syntax of his speech follows a maze-like movement

> where there is then no good
> For which to strive, no strife can grow up there
> From Faction; . . .
>
> (II.30-32)

Even more obviously word playing is

> Surer to prosper than prosperity
> Could have assur'd us; . . .
>
> (II.39-40)

26. Lewis, *A Preface to Paradise Lost*, p. 96.

It is the same technique he uses when he is persuading Eve to eat the apple:

> God therefore cannot hurt ye, and be just;
> Not just, not God; not fear'd then, nor obeyd:
> Your feare it self of Death removes the fear.
>
> (IX.700-702)

Verbal trickery is a constant feature of Satan's method. He introduces cannon into the war with a sustained sequence of puns. But his trickery has a noble tradition on Earth; he is compared to 'som Orator renownd / In *Athens* or free *Rome*' (IX.670-671). Once again he is like fallen man; once again, as with the devils' singing, technical brilliance is shown applied to an immoral purpose—making a further comment on the fallen world and the values of aesthetics and rhetoric.

Yet despite all the contrived and controlled brilliance of Satan's trickery, there is still the suspicion that he comes to believe in his own deceits and lies. It is possible that when he claims on his return to Hell that Night and Chaos had 'oppos'd / My journey strange' (X.478-479) he is simply lying for glory, and not deluded. But his conception of the universe and God's place in it is a deluded one. Continually he talks about 'hap' and 'chance' and 'fate': his opposition to God makes him rewrite a world picture in which events are not subject to God's control. God's rule is 'upheld by strength, or Chance, or Fate' (I.133) he claims. And chance, fate and hap are words that are continually associated with Satan's hopes.[27] That God controls everything in the universe of *Paradise Lost*—as we are shown in Book III—he refuses to believe. When he is finally approaching Eve, the whole group of words forms a maze which he finally cuts through to see her (IX.421ff.).

Satan's greatest self-deception is such a grandiose one that we might not even notice it, or consciously register it as an example of his delusion. From the beginning we are told the consequences for someone 'Who durst defie th' Omnipotent to Arms' (I.49). The impossibility—indeed stupidity—of defying the *Omnipotent* should be immediately apparent. Beelzebub confesses that he now thinks God is 'Almighty' (I.144) and Mammon's proposal to attack the Almighty with war is easily derided by Belial. But Satan's attack on the Almighty by stealth and secret cunning is still an attack on the Almighty, the Omnipotent.

We never, however, think this stupid. We are so used to the traditional heroic, the heroic band fighting great odds, that we think of terms like the 'almighty' and the 'omnipotent' merely as

27. Dennis H. Burden, *The Logical Epic* (1967), pp. 65ff., 93ff.

exaggerations. Indeed, we are expected to interpret the terms in that way—as if the devils are using the words carelessly. The terrible irony is that the terms are literally true. God is omnipotent, omniscient in the universe of *Paradise Lost*. We can still admire Satan and his followers for their heroism in tackling impossible odds—but these odds really are impossible. Their defiance is utterly futile. Yet it is a splendid delusion—far too splendid to be dismissed as stupid, as the doom of nonsense.

T. S. Eliot remarked that 'Milton's celestial and infernal regions are large but insufficiently furnished apartments filled by heavy conversation; and one remarks about the Puritan mythology its thinness.'[28] But Milton tried to supplement the thinness by augmentation from Hebrew and classical false gods, and Anglo-Saxon superstition (elves, for instance) to suggest a variety of devils in a variety of roles. One of the problems with Hell for Milton's poem was that as no one had yet died in the period covered by the action, it could not be filled with interesting figures—they are necessarily insufficiently furnished apartments. But Hell is not well furnished with tortures either. The penal fires become the fiery passions of the devils, and Satan's flames are both his punishment and his glory. There are some perfunctory classical tortures—but these are few, and Helen Gardner has perceptively commented

it is surely to Milton's credit that he showed so little inventiveness in imagining tortures or degrading the enemies of God and Man by showing them grotesquely deformed and contorted. He preferred to show the courage of his fallen angels in rising superior to fierce pain, without expatiating on the pain.[29]

His emphasis is not on God's vengeance (that is the God the devils 'create' for us in their comments) but on the goodness God will produce from evil; not on the tortures of Hell but on the bounty of the creation. The Hell that Milton portrays is a mental one. 'The mind is its own place.' When Satan utters that phrase, though, it is as a boast. He is:

> One who brings
> A mind not to be chang'd by Place or Time.
> The mind is its own place, and in it self
> Can make a Heav'n of Hell, a Hell of Heav'n.
> What matter where, if I be still the same,
>
> (I.252-256)

We do not doubt that he is steadfast, he will be still the same, he will not change. But because he will not change, he can never

28. T. S. Eliot, 'William Blake' in *Selected Essays* (1951), p. 321.
29. *A Reading of Paradise Lost*, pp. 45-6.

make a Heaven of Hell, can never make Hell other than Hell;
he is fixed in the state in which he fell when making a Hell of Heaven.
That was what he had threatened to Michael in the war: either
they would win 'Or turn this Heav'n it self into the Hell / Thou
fablest' (VI.291-292). Certainly the mind *is* its own place—but
for Satan this is not a retreat. He has vowed his mind will not change,
and his mind is the mental Hell he created in Heaven, and that he
will suffer eternally. 'What matters where, if I be still the same, . . .'

The aim of the rebellion was to be free of God. In Hell 'Here at
least / We shall be free' (I.258-259). But neither he nor the devils
can be free as their activity is utterly dependent on God's: the angels
obey God, the devils defy him—he is still the centre of their world:

> ever to do ill our sole delight,
> As being the contrary to his high will
> Whom we resist. . . .
>
> (I.160-163)

They are stuck in the rut of necessarily doing evil, necessarily
doing the opposite of whatever God does.

Satan's inner Hell is best brought out in Book IV. Here the full
irony of his defiant 'the mind is its own place' is demonstrated: it
is the mind that counts, no matter what the external circumstances;
but what seemed a boast in Hell is a doom in Paradise:

> for within him Hell
> He brings, and round about him, nor from Hell
> One step no more than from himself can fly
> By change of place: . . .
>
> (IV.20-23)

There is only one 'place' that matters, he has already announced.
His torment he confesses to in his first soliloquy—'Which way I
flie is Hell; my self am Hell' (IV.75). The Hell for him is now the
fact that he can never change: he knows—his soliloquy explains—
that if he were to repent, he would only fall again, so repentance is
impossible. As Abdiel told him earlier, 'Thy self not free, but to
thy self enthralld' (VI.181). Any place of bliss he visits he can
never experience—he can experience only Hell:

> But the hot Hell that always in him burnes,
> Though in mid Heav'n, soon ended his delight,
> And tortures him now more, the more he sees
> Of pleasure not for him ordaind: . . .
>
> (IX.467-470)

When he enters Paradise, his first words are 'O Hell' (IV.358).
It is a brilliant imaginative stroke of Milton's—and a brilliance the

41

greater since we realize that it is indeed inevitable (not just a flashy trick) that Satan should see and think of only Hell in Paradise. Paradise recreates Hell for him by reminding him of what happiness he misses—a reminder adding to his torments, part of his Hell; but also, in seeing Paradise he sees Hell again.

> With what delight could I have walkt thee round
> If I could joy in aught, sweet interchange
> Of Hill and Vallie, Rivers, Woods and Plains,
> Now Land, now Sea, and Shores with Forrest crownd,
> Rocks, Dens and Caves; but I in none of these
> Find place or refuge; and the more I see
> Pleasures about me, so much more I feel
> Torment within me, as from the hateful siege
> Of contraries; all good to me becomes
> Bane, and in Heav'n much worse would be my state.
>
> (IX.114-123)

It is a superbly rich passage, with its elegiac tone, its texture of echo and reminiscence, its tragic irony. His plan of 'out of good still to find means of evil' (I.165) has typically, inevitably, recoiled on him. Now, whenever he sees good, it becomes automatically evil and destructive to him. The greater the pleasure outside him, the more his mind suffers again the experience of Chaos—the 'torment' and 'hateful siege of contraries' instead of the peace known by Adam and Eve. He can find no 'place' here because for him 'the mind is its own place'—and his mind is Hell: place has become more than a colourless noun and carries now the implications of a fitting, proper appropriate place.[30] There is not such a place in Eden for him. As Raphael told Adam, Satan fell from Heaven 'Into his place' (VII.135).

Most striking in this speech, though, is the sudden echo of Hell's geography—'Rocks, Caves, Lakes, Fens, Bogs, Dens, and shades of death' (II.621). This is suddenly recalled in rhythm and vocabulary when Satan sees in Eden 'Rocks, Dens and Caves'. The reminiscence is brief; but it is significant. Even in a view of Eden Satan sees Hell, because carrying Hell within him, Hell is all he can know.

The echo suggests, too, that geographically Hell and Eden are similar. Hell has its 'many a dark and drearie Vale' (II.618), Eden has its 'sweet interchange / Of Hill and Vallie'. The difference is not geological, but in the mind. Satan carries Hell with him and what he sees is coloured by that. Eden is seen by Adam and Eve in their innocence so their minds interpret it as delightful. When they have sinned, Eden does not radically change—but their minds

---

30. *See* Isabel G. MacCaffrey, *Paradise Lost as 'Myth'* (1959), pp. 68-73.

do. Eden then seems to them menacing, they feel the need for clothes
—although they still look the same. The difference was in their
minds. Satan was quite right in insisting on the mind's primacy.
It can make a Heaven of Hell—except that with minds sworn
never to change, it never will. All Satan and the devils can do is
make a Hell of Heaven and Earth. He failed to realize how limited
and damned his mind was. 'One's country is wherever it is well
with one', Milton wrote in a letter to Peter Heimbach.[31] Ironically,
it is most well with Satan in Hell—that is where his mind is in
place, that is his country. Evil has become his good, what seems
ill is—he has insisted—for him well. He has come to need Hell for,
as he recognizes, 'in Heav'n much worse would be my state' (IX.123).

The debate in Hell is one of the great set pieces of *Paradise Lost*.
It is also fully functional. It sets the Fall of man in a cosmic framework,
makes it an event in the struggle between good and evil; and it
shows the planning of evil from which God will produce further good.
All this is shown, by the dramatization of the debate, in action.
Evil is not merely described, but we hear the voices of evil, see its
proponents hatching it.

The heroic grandeur of the fallen angels is presented in the heroic
grandeur of the verse, in the ideal political rhetoric. Mammon's
classic statement for splendid isolation is a piece of brilliant political
persuasion:

> Let us not then persue
> By force impossible, by leave obtain
> Unacceptable, though in Heav'n, our state
> Of splendid vassalage, but rather seek
> Our own good from our selves, and from our own
> Live to our selves, though in this vast recess,
> Free, and to none accountable, preferring
> Hard liberty before the easie yoke
> Of servile Pomp. . . .
>
> (II.249-257)

Cunningly he emphasizes the 'impossible', 'unacceptable'—the
verse resting on these words to insist that the devils cannot return
to Heaven; and the idea of their presence in Heaven is dismissed in a
throwaway parenthesis—'though in Heav'n'. He appeals to their
egotism, appeals to it as a politician appeals to a political nationalism
—'*Our own* good from *ourselves*, and from *our own*'. *Our* and *own* fill
the whole line—placed in its beginning, middle and end; it is an
appeal to 'us'—a national pride, national egotism; so that 'Hard

31. P. B. and E. M. W. Tillyard (eds), *Private Correspondence and Academic Exercises*
(1932), p. 51.

43

liberty' becomes not, as it might have been put, something unpleasant, but something worth striving for. Because it is 'hard', therefore it is good.

Politically the debate is as ambivalent as everything else in Hell. The rhetoric of the speeches is nobly impressive; yet the inner council was of a 'thousand Demi-Gods on golden seats' (I.796) which presents not only something bigger and greater than the world could ever achieve, but also, as Merritt Hughes pointed out something that would have seemed to Milton a travesty of parliamentary government. [32] Disregarding the ambivalence, various critics have tried to see in the debate references to Cromwell and to Charles I. To try to identify Satan with one or the other positively is of course ridiculous; but the more general point, that the devils are like fallen man and so mirror man's political activities, is true. Our admiration of the debate, however, must be tempered by remembering the associations of Satan with political tyranny.

It is from Hell, and especially from the debate in Hell, that we get our first ideas about Heaven in the poem. *Paradise Lost* opens in Hell: so structurally there is an enactment of the 'good from evil' theme when we leave the scenes in Hell for those in Heaven. Moreover, the opening in Hell is appropriate for the reader's condition as fallen man; he will understand fallen angels more readily than unfallen angels at first. So our first ideas of Heaven come through the Devil's comments and actions in trying to regain or imitate Heaven; just as in Book IV our first view of Paradise is through Satan's eyes. It is through the comments and vision of the fallen that we must approach perfection.

The devils express an ambivalent attitude towards God. He is the hated tyrant of 'rage' and 'wrauth' who 'sole reigning holds the Tyranny of Heav'n' as Satan says (I.95, 110, 124). Yet at the same time the might and supremacy of Providence is, as G. A. Wilkes has shown, [33] constantly attested, not only by the defeat of the rebels and by the misery they are plunged into, but by the way they involuntarily refer to God as 'Heav'ns perpetual King', 'Almighty', 'th'Omnipotent', 'th'Almighty' (I.131, 144, 273, 623) and, in the course of the debate, as 'Heav'ns Lord supream', 'Heav'ns all-ruling Sire', 'Heav'ns high Arbitrator' (II.236, 264, 359).

The first indication we get of the way in which divine providence works comes from Satan: 'If then his Providence / Out of our evil seek to bring forth good' (I.162-163). From Belial in the debate comes the suggestion that God may relent (II.210ff.). The devils are not ignorant of God's goodness and mercy. Moreover, the beauty,

32. Merritt Hughes, *Ten Perspectives on Milton* (1965), p. 187.
33. G. A. Wilkes, *The Thesis of 'Paradise Lost'* (1961), pp. 11-12.

44

serenity, happiness and perfection of Heaven are constantly being established, partly in the narrative—'th'ethereal Skie', 'the Crystal Battlements' (I.45, 742)—but especially in the devils' own comments in the debate. Belial refers to 'th'Ethereal mould / Incapable of stain' (II.139-140) and Mammon refers scathingly to God breathing 'Ambrosial Odours and Ambrosial Flowers' (II.245), not because these odours and scents that are offered to God are contemptible, but because they would have to be 'servile offerings'. Satan's conclusion of the debate is with the hope of reaching somewhere 'Nearer our ancient Seat' (II.394ff.). The reluctance of the devils to admit the desirability of Heaven can easily be imagined; that nevertheless they do make these admissions must be a mark of great goodness of Heaven, and the power of God.

Most convincing of all evidence that the devils recognize the desirability of Heaven, is their need to imitate it. Mammon gives the plan concisely:

> As he our Darkness, cannot we his Light
> Imitate when we please? This Desert soile
> Wants not her hidden lustre, Gemms and Gold;
> Nor want we skill or art, from whence to raise
> Magnificence; and what can Heav'n shew more?
>
> (II.269-273)

It is a fine example of Milton's skill in dramatizing a character; not only does the conversation further the action, it reveals admirably Mammon's fallen nature. God can imitate the Devil's darkness as he is omnipotent; the devils are not—that is why (to answer the rhetorical question that expected no answer) they cannot imitate his light. It is not the only reason, though: Mammon's concentration on material splendour prevents him from ever conceiving that God's light is not merely a physical phenomenon, but an expression of moral worth. The devils are in darkness, and Satan's radiance has faded, because they are morally corrupt. Without the basic moral qualities, the physical features that are expressions of that basis, cannot be obtained. It is this again that Mammon fails to understand in his 'and what can Heav'n shew more?' The 'hidden lustre' he refers to will always be 'hidden', not just because it is at the moment underground, but because without any moral basis for it, it can never shine like Heaven's. And Heaven is nothing like the artificially lit Hell: his comparison is absurd, not only because in physical appearance Heaven can show a lot more, but also because the comparison is an irrelevant one. It is not on the basis of gems and jewels that Heaven is to be assessed. Mammon, fallen, will never see that.

The attempt to imitate Heaven by building Pandæmonium shows both the need of the devils to regain a Heaven, and their infinite distance from it. Their imitation can never be like the real thing. And their corruption is shown in imagining that it can be. No longer aware of the moral basis to Heaven's light, they become in some ways content with Hell.

The very fact of their imitating Heaven is a presumption. Satan sits on a throne parodying God. His pride and corruption are testified to in this; the details of the comparison show even further how unlike God he is. Satan sits 'from despair / Thus high uplifted beyond hope' (II.6-7), whereas God 'sits / High Thron'd above all highth' (III.57-58). Satan is perched as if by an Indian rope trick on thoroughly insubstantial foundations: God sits transcending finite measurement or support.

From their corrupt presumptuousness the devils attempt to imitate Heaven, but in their failure to imitate it successfully, in producing only a parody, they testify to their own corruption again. The angels in Heaven are ranked in circular perfection:

> in Orbs
> Of circuit inexpressible they stood,
> Orb within Orb, . . .

> (V.594-596)

The devils in imitating the heavenly organization cannot achieve this perfection. Satan prepared

> To speak; whereat thir doubl'd Ranks they bend
> From Wing to Wing, and half enclose him round

> (I.616-617)

Because they are fallen they are unable—or do not know how—to express perfection. They can manage only a semi-circle.

But as Satan has already decided on a policy of perverse parody of God's redemption—'ever to do ill our sole delight' (I.160)—it could be that the devils have renounced symbols of perfection, and adopted for themselves symbols of imperfection. 'Evil be thou my Good' (IV.110). Hence they *have* to rank themselves in a semi-circle in opposition to the circular ranks of the angels. The tragic irony is, of course, that though they may think this is a voluntary decision on their part in defying God, and his values, in fact they are now incapable of achieving perfection. There is no choice for them.

The parody scheme of *Paradise Lost* is an intricate and complex one. Perhaps the most grotesque example is that of the infernal Trinity made by Satan, Sin, and Death. As Sin says to Satan:

46

                At they right hand voluptuous, as beseems
                Thy daughter and thy darling, without end.
                                                    (II.868-870)

Is this the nearest Satan can ever get to imitating the Trinity of God?
Or is it a deliberately grotesque insult, a contemptuous parody, a
sort of black mass? The two possibilities are not separable. Satan's
hatred of God is so great that imitation must involve not love but
insult; and his corruption is so great that his imitations must always
be grotesquely different from their original; he must always 'pervert'
(and it is his own word—I.164) God's goodness.

   Through the first two books, then, we get a picture of Heaven—
an inverted, parody picture. It was a dangerous device used in the
way Milton used it. He begins with the parody, and the object
parodied is kept from us until the third book. The danger is that
Heaven, when we get to it, will seem to be parodying Hell. By
beginning the poem in Hell, the acts of Heaven seem only to be
the response called out by the energies of Hell, as Helen Gardner
has pointed out.[34] Certainly Milton's intention was to show how
Providence produced good from evil. As G. A. Wilkes indicates,
'Books I and II have presented Satan's plan of action: Book III
predicts God's counterstroke, through which the fall will be made
productive of even greater good than would have been possible
without it'.[35] The thesis is clear enough: the fall of the angels produces the good of the creation; and the ensuing fall of man produces
the good of the redemption. That is the celestial cycle, yet there
remains the suspicion, encouraged by beginning the poem in Hell,
and based on the mystery of the whole myth, that God is not often
spontaneously good. Good will follow evil—but why can't there be
good without evil? Indeed, *can* there be good without evil? Implications of dualism hover around the poem.

34. *A Reading of Paradise Lost*, p. 213.
35. *The Thesis of 'Paradise Lost'*, p. 16.

CHAPTER III

Heaven

It might be argued that Book III of *Paradise Lost* is the most important. On the success or failure of this initial presentation of God and Heaven, hangs the success or failure of the whole poem. To 'assert Eternal Providence, / And justifie the wayes of God to men' (I.25-26), Milton must successfully establish God, must give a coherent and convincing account of his theological scheme at its node. The whole 'great Argument' depends on this book.

There is no critical agreement on the success of this book, nor indeed on the entire presentation of God. Moreover, even amongst those who agree that the presentation is successful, there is not agreement as to where the success lies: for instance, John M. Diekhoff has defended Milton's scheme from a Christian standpoint in *Milton's Paradise Lost* (1946), while William Empson in *Milton's God* (1961) has defended the consistency and coherence of the scheme with the conclusion that 'the poem is so good because it makes God so bad'.

However, it might be argued that Milton was concerned with the theme stated in his title, with Paradise lost, with what was lost, and how—but not why. He explains why it is lost in terms of Adam and Eve's disobedience and Satan's temptation, but is not concerned with the theological basis of the myth—is not concerned 'with Providence, Foreknowledge, Will, and Fate, / Fixt Fate, free Will, Foreknowledge absolute'. He leaves that maze alone in order to present the image of deprivation and exile, the loss of Paradise. That (in such an account) would be the imaginative heart of the poem, not the theology.

To describe and picture Heaven was a difficult task. Milton first begins to establish it by contrasting it with Hell, to which it is so different, so superior. If in the first two books the devils build magnificence, Heaven is infinitely better we realize in Book III, not iust in what it contains but in what it lacks—flames and ice, whirlwinds, volcanoes and such disruptive features. Similarly the description of Hell is helped because of the continual contrasts, explicit and implicit, with Heaven: it can only be a pale shadow of Heaven, a derisory imitation. With the conjuring trick of this relativistic comparison, Milton is able to suggest two contrasting but unknown places.

For Hell he could make earthly comparisons in the similes: the fallen angels are like man. But to compare Heaven with things of man would be indecorous—as well as totally inaccurate. So we lack, in the scenes in Heaven, the comparisons with earthly places and events that we find so often in Hell and Paradise. Similarly, there are few of the traditional sustained epic similes that we found in the opening books; they are no longer appropriate. Instead, Milton suggests that Heaven not only transcends any physical place, but that it is totally unlike one. Physical dimensions and descriptions are inapplicable. Our first sight of it—through Satan's eyes, as with Paradise—is a brief, suggestive glimpse:

> Farr off th' Empyreal Heav'n, extended wide
> In circuit, undetermined square or round,
> With Opal Towrs and Battlements adornd
> Of living Saphire, once his native Seat;
>
> (II.1047-1050)

Its beauty is attested in the brief visual image, but emphasized not by picture but emotion. 'Once his native Seat' evokes the fact of Satan's current exile, of his exclusion from bliss now—suggesting that the beauty that is lost is so much keener. It is this emotional response that catches the beauty of Heaven, rather than the detail of the picture: 'living Saphire' is an attempt to suggest the super-natural—organic jewels analagous to the 'vegetable Gold' of unfallen Paradise (IV.220), not the dead stones of the fallen world or of Hell—where they are found in 'Desert soile' (II.270-271). But 'living Saphire' is not an imaginative way of expressing the mystery—it merely states and does not offer any imaginative perception of what this wonderful growth of jewel can be. There is no emotional suggestiveness in it.

Yet Milton does catch the transcendence of earthly limitations in this description of Heaven. The 'Battlements' may worry us with Manichaean questions—does God need them to keep out Satan? Is he not omnipotent? But 'undetermined square or round' does suggest how Heaven is not limited to earthly rules. Milton takes his image from geometry: though no earthly mathematician can square the circle, Heaven is an example of the two shapes in one. Milton suggests the mystery and transcendental nature of Heaven here, and suggests it by an almost metaphysical conceit. It is a wit

49

not often present in the descriptions of Heaven, but that recurs importantly in some of the details of the creation.

To describe the indescribable, Milton resorts to paradox—like 'liquid Pearl' (III.519). But not only does this fail to evoke much mystery and wonder, it is also too like Hell. The paradoxes themselves are not the same as those of Hell, but the rhetorical device of paradox is one that has been firmly established as part of the world of Hell in the first two books—'No light, but rather darkness visible' (I.63), 'life dies, death lives' (II.624). Hell as a place of moral confusion and contradiction, of mazes and will-o'-the-wisps, is well described by oxymoron, but to use the same device for the moral positive of Heaven is less satisfactory. Can Milton afford to be enigmatic about Heaven as well as about Hell? Doesn't he need to be positive about one to make the moral point of contrast?

Eventually, indeed, Milton confesses that Heaven is indescribable by fallen man—and appropriately it is a vision seen through the eyes of the fallen Satan that provokes this reaction.

> The work as of a Kingly Palace Gate
> With Frontispice of Diamond and Gold
> Imbellisht, thick with sparkling orient Gemms
> The Portal shon, inimitable on Earth
> By Model, or by shading Pencil drawn.
>
> (III.505-509)

It is as much a confession of defeat as an evocation of the inexpressible. Visual description of Heaven is, Milton concedes, impossible. It is a mark of his tact and intelligence that he tries it so rarely, and offers us instead a series of pregnant hints.

Milton evokes Heaven less by description than by traditional images of order and harmony. The groups of images were conventional enough, and full accounts of them can be found in such studies as C. S. Lewis' *The Discarded Image* and E. M. W. Tillyard's *The Elizabethan World Picture*. The idea that the creation of the world was an act of music, or that the created universe was in a state of music, were ideas commonplace to the seventeenth century. The order of the universe was expressed by, and performed to, music, and the movement of the heavenly bodies was a dance. It is to this order that the angels are compared, after God has elevated his Son. The angels

> That day, as other solemn days, they spent
> In song and dance about the sacred Hill,
> Mystical dance, which yonder starrie Spheare
> Of Planets and of fixt in all her Wheeles
> Resembles nearest, mazes intricate,

> Eccentric, intervolv'd, yet regular
> Then most, when most irregular they seem:
> And in thir motions harmonie Divine
> So smooths her charming tones, that Gods own eare
> Listens delighted. Ev'ning now approachd
> (For wee have also our Ev'ning and our Morn,
> Wee ours for change delectable, not need)
> Forthwith from dance to sweet repast they turn
> Desirous; all in Circles as they stood,
> Tables are set, . . .
>
> (V.618-632)

Just as the universe revolves in regular order, in circular motion, so do the angels dance; the circle implies a perfection. In the apocalyptic conclusion to *Of Reformation* (1641), Milton foresaw the time when the good men of earth 'in supereminence of beatific vision, progressing the dateless and irrevoluble circle of eternity, shall clasp inseparable hands with joy and bliss, in overmeasure for ever'.[1]

The orderly dance is an image of perfection. Before the Fall Earth is, as Satan remarks, a—

> Terrestrial Heav'n, danc't round by other Heav'ns
> That shine, yet bear thir bright officious Lamps,
> Light above Light, for thee alone, as seems,
>
> (IX.103-105)

Here a further image of goodness, that of light, augments the image of the orderly movement of the universe, its circular, regular dance. Just as God's sacred Hill is the centre to the angels' circular dance, so is Earth to the planets' dance. Such a description, of course, depends on an acceptance of the Ptolemaic conception of a stationary Earth around which the planets revolve. Milton, however, was aware of the Copernican theory that the Earth moved like other celestial bodies around the sun, and both theories are presented by Raphael to Adam (VIII.66-178). So Milton can present the scientifically more current theory as well as retain the poetically and theologically traditional one. To have adopted fully and solely the Copernican theory would have required a reduction in the importance of the world if the theory of circular dance and perfection was to be retained. Milton's symbolism of order was obsolescent at the time he was using it.

The angels in their dance also sing—just as traditionally the

---

1. *Of Reformation In England And the Causes that Hitherto Have Hindered It*, in Burton, p. 52. 'Irrevoluble' here means having no finite period of revolution, of infinite circuit.

planets sang in their movements. From Plato on throughout Renaissance literature, the idea recurs. Milton's 'At a Solemn Music', tells how man's sin lost him the ability to join in reply to the music of the spheres.

Milton adopts this concept of the music of the spheres, and allies it to the scriptural suggestions of a musical Heaven—angelic choirs singing to the harp. The result is a system of his own in which, as Spaeth puts it in his valuable study, 'the universal harmony has as its object the praise of the Creator, and in which the spheres join in some mysterious fashion with Christian spirits and angels to produce a complete concord, inaudible to man until he shall succeed in escaping from the bonds of sin'.[2]

And so we find the cosmic dance allied with music. When Raphael suggests that the sun is centre of the universe, he suggests too that the other stars 'dance about him various rounds' (VIII.125). The dance of circular movement ('round') is here, but rounds are also songs. Adam in his prayer is quite explicit when he refers to planets that 'move / In mystic Dance not without Song' (V.177-178).

Milton continually indicates the musical nature of the universe and the unfallen world by punning—as if to suggest by 'rounds' for instance that a round dance automatically and necessarily involves a round song. He tells of the Firmament with 'all her numberd Starrs, that seem to roule / Spaces incomprehensible' (VIII.19-20), and how the constellations 'move / Thir Starry dance in numbers that compute / Days, months, and years' (III.579-581). He is punning upon numbers in both cases; in the first, on the fact that God knows how many are the countless stars, in the second on the numbers of days and months in the calendar of time—and in each passage there is the associated meaning of 'numbers' as the numbers of music—reminding us that the stars sing.

The other major image of order that Milton used is that of the Great Chain of Being—a conception of the different sorts of minerals, plants, and animals ranged in order above and below each other—man superior to the animals, angels superior to man. The chain reached finally to the foot of God's throne. Raphael explains it to Adam.

> O *Adam*, one Almightie is, from whom
> All things proceed, and up to him return,
> If not deprav'd from good, created all
> Such to perfection, one first matter all,
> Indu'd with various forms, various degrees
> Of substance, and in things that live, of life;
> But more refin'd, more spiritous and pure,

2. Sigmund Spaeth, *Milton's Knowledge of Music* (1913), p. 69.

As nearer to him plac't or nearer tending
Each in thir several active Sphears assignd,
Till body up to spirit work, in bounds
Proportiond to each kind. . . .

(V.469-479)

This description of the order of nature produced naturally the concept of hierarchy. The groups of life were arranged in order on the chain (plants, fish, animals, birds, etc.), and within the groups the individual members were arranged, too, in order of superiority. The lion (or sometimes the elephant) was supreme amongst the beasts, the whale (or sometimes the dolphin) amongst the fishes. (So when Satan is like a whale and a lion—I.201, IV.402—his power is being affirmed.) The scheme applied not only to living matter: the sun was supreme amongst the stars, justice amongst the virtues, the head amongst the body's members and, as Raphael makes clear (V.487) reason amongst the mind's faculties. The universe was constructed on a principle of hierarchy, and an observance and acceptance of it were good.

So we have the complex types of angels in Heaven (copied, too, by the devils). God summons them—

Hear all ye Angels, Progenie of Light,
Thrones, Dominations, Princedoms, Vertues, Powers,

(V.600-601)

This is not merely Milton's 'organ voice' delighting in the noise of words; the essential, hierarchical nature of Heaven is being insisted upon. The concept is not merely asserted but dramatized, as Lewis points out: Milton 'delights in the ceremonious interchange of unequal courtesies, with condescension (a beautiful word which we have spoiled) on the one side and reverence on the other'.[3] So the heavenly world is created in action.

When God speaks to his Son—

He said, and on his Son with Rays direct
Shon full: he all his Father full exprest
Ineffably into his face receiv'd,

(VI.719-721)

Some of the effect here comes from the pun, that God shines implicitly like the sun on to his Son, who receives a secondary radiance like the moon. God is elsewhere compared implicitly to the sun; to compare him directly to the sun would be contravening the decorum of the Chain of Being. Satan can be compared to the sun as it ennobles him, but God is superior to everything so to compare him to the

3. C. S. Lewis, *A Preface to Paradise Lost* (1942), p. 79.

sun would be insulting rather than ennobling. However, an implicit comparison, by suggesting tacitly and tactfully that God is like the supreme star, like (in one system of astronomy) the centre of the universe, reminds us that God is light, and suggests some of his magnificence. And with the implicit sun-moon image, the hierarchical positions God and Christ bear to each other are suggested naturally—positions that are dramatically shown in the interchange of courtesies. For Christ replies with due deference—'So said, hee ore his Scepter bowing, rose' (VI.746). Imagery, formal speech and gesture derive their force from the hierarchical concept. To be aware of it is to realize that the heavenly exchanges and ranks are not merely empty verbiage or 'heavy conversation', but dramatic images of the order of Heaven.

It is fortunately hard for us to accept this conception now. It led obviously to a view of the world as the best of all possible worlds when everyone and everything observed its proper place. It led naturally to the idea of 'The rich man in his castle, the poor man at the gate' which is not a debasement of the idea, but a logical application of it: 'Each in their several active Spheres assigned'— and God assigned that the poor should be poor and the rich rich. The idea of the Chain of Being with its concomitant system of hierarchy was a great force for conservatism: the woman is naturally inferior to man, some races are naturally superior to others. And of course anyone who rebelled against this system rebelled against God who had laid it down, and who was at the top of the chain or ladder. Satan rebelled in this way. 'He felt himself impaired' by having Christ elevated above him. He should have, according to the hierarchical concept, accepted that whatever God did was right, and that the right place for Satan was the place he was in, and one inferior to God. Our sympathy for Satan comes from our admiration for someone refusing to accept a static social order. It may be an unhistoric admiration, and the seventeenth-century reader may have been more shocked at Satan's acting against the natural order of things than admiring of his dynamic rebellion against authoritarianism. But the modern reader will never be able to read with seventeenth-century eyes on this point. Yet the mid-seventeenth century did see something of a change in attitude to a hierarchical society. After the Restoration, certainly, conservatism and conformity were the order. But during the Civil War and the Interregnum there did arise the Diggers and the Levellers with their movement towards egalitarianism, during this period women did achieve some increase in independence. And the idea of degree, of keeping one's proper station, also underwent modification.[4]

4. *See* Christopher Hill, *The Century of Revolution* (1961), p. 92.

In contrast to the darkness of Hell, Heaven is presented as a place of light. The darkness of Hell indicated that it was a place of evil, and deeds of evil are done at night: Satan is compared to a wolf waiting 'at Eve' for the penned sheep, (IV.183ff.) and to the will-o'-the-wisp misleading 'th'amaz'd Night-wanderer' (IX.640). It is at night, in her dream inspired by Satan, that Eve is first tempted (V.30ff.). But Heaven is a place of light, and God is described in terms of light—

> since God is Light,
> And never but in unapproached Light
> Dwelt from Eternitie, . . .

(III.3-5)

The immediate source, of course, is the first epistle of St John: 'God is light, and in him is no darkness at all' (I.5), but Milton's treatment of the idea derives also from Plotinus, and perhaps Manichaeism, to its ultimate source in the allegory of the cave in Plato's *Republic*.[5] As with his imagery of order and harmony, he combines the Biblical and Platonic. The light is an image of moral worth, of goodness, and an image, too, of intellectual understanding: 'God is the lord which hath shewed us light' (Psalm 118:27). 'Enlightener of my darkness', Adam calls Michael (XII.271). The fallen angels, without faith, without understanding, are plunged into 'utter darkness'.

The simplicity of the scheme of the contrast between light and dark, running throughout the poem, makes it easy to undervalue. Because it is so simple and so traditional an image, it achieves its success. When Eliot acknowledged that 'to me it seems that Milton is at his best in imagery suggestive of vast size, limitless space, abysmal depth, and light and darkness',[6] he was acknowledging Milton's success in those metaphorical structures that are basic to the poem.

Like the imagery of order, the imagery of light is a way of presenting God and Heaven in terms other than anthropomorphic ones. And it is jointly visual and evaluative—creating both a picture and a moral judgement. The beauty, serenity, purity, goodness of Heaven are simultaneously conveyed.

There is a danger of an implied dualism, of a suggestion of the eternal struggle between light and dark. In the world as we know it night and day can be seen as balancing forces, so the image suggests that God and Satan are equal. Indeed there was during, and after, Milton's time at Cambridge, considerable interest there in Zoro-astrianism with its belief that the cosmic battle is between light and

5. Irene Samuel, *Plato and Milton* (1947), p. 39.
6. T. S. Eliot, 'Milton II' in *On Poetry and Poets* (1957), p. 156.

dark as equally divine aspects of God. Milton, though, generally avoids this speculation by making it clear in other contexts, in other images and in the action, that Satan is nothing like equal to God.

However, God sometimes seems like Satan, the light imagery suggests. When Mammon claimed in Hell that God often chose to reside 'amidst / Thick clouds and dark' (II.263-264) it seemed merely a Hellish lie. Yet the angels hymn God saying 'Dark with excessive bright thy skirts appear' (III.380). God's brightness is given a Hellish colouration—and, it seems, a Hellish moral evaluation.

But it is a Hellish colouration for man only. The passage reminds us of St Paul's 'Through a glass darkly'. God's behaviour seems to be dark—both dark and mysterious and dark and cruel—because of our imperfect vision, because our minds cannot approach or understand his radiance. It is like looking—and Milton's imagery implies this—directly at the bright sun; we see a blackness. But that is not in the object we are looking at, it is in the inadequacy of our eyes (and of angelic eyes, seemingly). As Milton wrote in *Of Reformation in England*, 'The very essence of truth is plainess and brightness; the darkness and crookedness is our own'.[7]

The Manichaean suggestions in *Paradise Lost* emanate mainly from Satan. He does think that God is another figure like himself, a rival whom he can overthrow, and he tries to equal God by mimicking his throne, his hierarchical system of followers, his Trinity. But whereas God has some anthropomorphic features, Satan is limited to anthropomorphism. His acts are like man's and differ only in degree—in strength, in skill, in size; or in some angelic spiritual qualities he still retains—in being able to change his shape and form (I.423-431). Yet even when he uses this spiritual quality of changing shape, it is always to fulfil some aim that he is performing in a human way; he still has to persuade Eve verbally to eat the fruit, even though he has a disguise.

God, however, is omnipotent and omniscient; he has no need for such devices of shape changing, he is not limited like Satan. Whereas we see Satan always active, always doing something, always moving, God does not move—he has no need to. Satan's plan for the seduction of mankind is a long campaign of planning, journeying, spying and persuasion; but 'Immediat are the Acts of God, more swift / Than time or motion' (VII.176-7). To show the futility of Satan's rebellion against God, these divine qualities of God are emphasized in various ways. Our first encounter with him shows his *difference* from Satan—something that needs to be emphasized after the plans of emulation and rivalry in the first two books.

7. Burton, p. 23.

Now had th' Almighty Father from above,
From the pure Empyrean where he sits
High Thron'd above all highth, bent down his eye,
His own works and their works at once to view:
About him all the Sanctities of Heaven
Stood thick as Starrs, and from his sight receiv'd
Beatitude past utterance; on his right
The radiant image of his Glory sat
His onely Son: On Earth he first beheld
Our two first Parents, yet the onely two
Of mankind, in the happie Garden plac't,
Reaping immortal fruits of joy and love,
Uninterrupted joy, unrivald love
In blissful solitude; he then surveyd
Hell and the Gulf between, and *Satan* there
Coasting the wall of Heav'n on this side Night
In the dun Air sublime, and ready now
To stoop with wearied wings and willing feet
On the bare outside of this World, that seemd
Firm land imbosomd without Firmament,
Uncertain which, in Ocean or in Air.
Him God beholding from his prospect high,
Wherein past, present, future he beholds,
Thus to his onely Son foreseeing spake.

(III.56-79)

God is presented here as observing the action of man and the Devil;
observing from outside, not competing in the struggle on their terms.
He is, 'High Thron'd above all highth' suggests, somewhere both
higher than and also outside of earthly, finite measurements. He is not
merely in the highest possible place, but higher than any possible
place—because of his moral worth, his being the summit of the whole
Chain of Being; and because he is so high he is at a vantage point
of being able to see everything. Beyond finite measurements, he is
outside the universe. The 'Empyrean' is the *coelum empyraeum*, the
sphere of the cosmos beyond the bounds of the fixed stars, outside
the created universe. The name signifies fire: since fire was the best
of the elements, and heavenly fire better than elemental, the highest
perfection was symbolized. And the idea of God as light, suggested
by fire, is augmented by the 'Sanctities of Heaven' described as
'thick as starrs' receiving beatitude from him—like stars receiving
light.[8]

Moving inwards from Heaven in the Empyrean, there were nine
spheres revolving around the Earth. Man is subject to the innermost,
the moon's sphere—that furthest from perfection. The moon's

8. *See* E. M. W. Tillyard, *The Elizabethan World Picture* (1943), p. 35.

sphere is one of mutability, changefulness and uncertainty. God, looking down from his perfection beyond the spheres, is able to see with complete clarity. Man, living in the thicker air of the sublunary sphere, is limited in his sight and understanding.

Unlimited by earthly measurements or earthly sight, God looks down on the limited beings, created by him, Satan, Adam and Eve. The former is struggling, moving, wearied: Adam and Eve are in complete peace. But both the restlessness and the rest are conditions of humans or angels—God is unlike either.

God is superior to his created beings in not being limited to time. Mankind and the Devil are limited by it, their acts take time, they exist only in the present. But God can see 'past, present, future' together. Milton not only states this, he shows it in the verse. 'In eternitie there is no distinction of Tenses' Sir Thomas Browne wrote[9]—and Milton shows God's transcendence of time by tense shifts within this paragraph: 'had . . . bent down', 'sits', 'stood', 'beholds . . . foreseeing spake'. He said in the past what in the present he sees will happen in the future. There is a similar sort of condensation in the line 'His own works and their works at once to view', where he simultaneously sees (and the condensation of the line enforces the simultaneity) what creatures he has made, and what things his creatures will make or have made.

This whole panoramic vision is one of Milton's brilliancies. It places for the reader the different strands of the plot in their relation to each other at this point in the story. Yet it is more than merely a narrative device, it is our first vision of God, one that shows his superiority to the limited Satan, shows his omniscience, and shows his foreknowledge. By seeing God's omniscience we see both God, and the state of the poem's action. The great spatial expanse is evoked for us to establish again the great sweep of the action, the immensity of the universe that is involved: yet it is an expanse immediately and simply apperceivable to God—so that his omnipotence and omniscience are demonstrated by the fact that he can grasp it in this one vision.

By imagery of light and order, by attributes of omniscience and omnipotence, by transcendence of time and place, God is created as a supreme force rather than an anthropomorphic personality. Even his speech is not a human tongue, as Broadbent has pointed out: 'he juggles with a limited number of arbitrary words, meanings and syntactical shapes'.[10] God's first speech is not personal, but the abstract word, the logos—so another Biblical abstraction is used, God as the word as well as God as light, to describe the indescribable.

9. *The Works of Sir Thomas Browne* (ed. G. Keynes, 1964), I.20.
10. J. B. Broadbent, *Some Graver Subject* (1960), p. 146.

Satan's rhetoric has been moving, personal, impassioned. God has to be a contrast with Satan's voice and a denial of the God the devils have 'created' in the first two books, the malignant tyrant; he has to be not an individual competing with Satan in a debate, but a totally different impersonal creation. This is established in his first speech, as Irene Samuel has shown:

> The near tonelessness of his first speech at once proves itself the right tone. It has offended readers because they assume that the 'I' who speaks is or should be a person like other persons. The flat statement of fact, past, present, and future, the calm analysis and judgment of deeds and principles —these naturally strike the ear that has heard Satan's ringing utterance as cold and impersonal. They should. For the omniscient voice of the omnipotent moral law speaks simply what it is. Here is no orator using rhetoric to persuade, but the nature of things expounding itself in order to present fact and principle unadorned.[11]

Some of the objections that God is too legalistic in *Paradise Lost* can be countered by realizing that God *is* the law and that his voice is the 'toneless voice of the moral law'.[12]

However, although some of the typical objections that Milton's God is cold, impersonal, legalistic can be countered by an understanding of Milton's concern to de-personalize him, not all his features can be explained in this way. Certainly as Basil Willey has written 'the whole effort of theology for centuries, and particularly in the seventeenth century, had been to avoid the contradictions which result from conceiving of God pictorially as a magnified human potentate'.[13] Yet Milton seems to have chosen to represent him as such a magnified human potentate in *Paradise Lost*: the abstract qualities are there—but so are the anthropomorphic ones.

The demands of putting God into an epic poem encouraged the portrayal of a personal, anthropomorphic deity. As Willey puts it, 'God had to be *deemed* omnipresent, omniscient, omnipotent and benevolent, yet *portrayed* as localized in Heaven'.[14] But it was not merely from writing an epic poem that Milton resorted to this presentation. The Old Testament God is often anthropomorphic, so obviously is Christ in the New Testament: Milton has a tradition of the personal God. His first speech, however, opens with something of the impersonal toneless voice mentioned earlier.

11. Irene Samuel, 'The Dialogue in Heaven', *Publications of the Modern Language Association of America*, LXXII (1957), 601-11.
12. Samuel, 'The Dialogue in Heaven', *Publications of the Modern Language Association of America*, LXXII (1957), 601-11.
13. Basil Willey, *The Seventeenth Century Background* (1934), p. 252.
14. Willey, *The Seventeenth Century Background*, p. 252.

> Onely begotten Son, seest thou what rage
> Transports our adversarie, whom no bounds
> Prescrib'd, no barrs of Hell, nor all the chains
> Heap't on him there, nor yet the main Abyss
> Wide interrupt can hold; . . .

(III.80-84)

One of the difficulties of Milton's theme was that if God could see, foresee and know everything, his remarking on it could only be superfluous. He is describing the obvious: it is even worse when Christ tells God things; such conversations are pointless—they can only be repeating what God has foreseen earlier. The problem is perhaps insoluble, and Milton does not at all minimize it by putting in phrases like 'seest thou' as if to make it more 'realistic'. Christ can see and is seeing Satan—God is not even indicating something Christ has not noticed; the phrase is redundant. It moreover draws attention to the dialogue as conversation, so emphasizing the inherent difficulties and contradictions.

If we accept that God is 'the word', presenting unadorned fact, undistorted, uncoloured, truth, some of the difficulties are temporarily shelved. He is not engaging in conversation in order to inform someone, but giving word to facts since he is the word. The need to present the simple, true word would then explain what Daiches has called the 'tactless literalism' that 'leads Milton to make God address His Son by his full Christian theological title'.[15] 'Onely begotten Son' parallels the heroics of those introductory epithets by which the devils address each other. It seems rather tame and banal and self-evident, unless we accept the idea of God as word speaking the unadorned truth, contrasting with and surpassing, for instance, the devilish flattery of 'O Prince, O Chief of many Throned Powers' (I.128).

Yet if God is the abstract, true impersonal word, what are we then to make of his account of Satan's escape from Hell? He claims nothing can hold him there, yet earlier we were given a different version:

> So stretcht out huge in length the Arch-fiend lay
> Chaind on the burning Lake, nor ever thence
> Had ris'n or heav'd his head, but that the will
> And high permission of all-ruling Heaven
> Left him at large to his own dark designs,
> That with reiterated crimes he might
> Heap on himself damnation, . . .

(I.209-215)

15. David Daiches, *Milton* (2nd rev. edn, 1959), p. 181.

This version is in keeping with God's omnipotence, although it creates problems of God's cruelty—which we find again in Book III when God talks of Satan's revenge 'that shall redound / Upon his own rebellious head' (III.85-86). But the two accounts of the escape contradict each other.

That Milton should contradict himself from forgetfulness, and make a contradiction denying God's omnipotence is not at all likely. Tillyard suggests that God is being ironical and mocking Satan.[16] This is certainly in character with God. However, when God does speak ironically, his irony is indicated explicitly. There is the striking passage before the war where God is talking, again to Christ:

> Nearly it now concernes us to be sure
> Of our Omnipotence, and with what Arms
> We mean to hold what anciently we claim
> Of Deitie or Empire, such a foe
> Is rising, who intends to erect his Throne
> Equal to ours, . . .
>
> Let us advise, and to this hazard draw
> With speed what force is left, and all imploy
> In our defence, lest unawares we lose
> This our high place, our Sanctuarie, our Hill.
>
> (V.721-726, 729-732)

It is a disturbing passage; suddenly we see confirmed Satan's account that God 'from the terror of this Arm so late / Doubted his Empire' (I.113-114). But our surprise is deliberately cultivated; we are misled just as Satan was, into believing that God is in doubt. It obviously suits Milton's purpose that we fallen readers should fall into the same trap as Satan—and he does not seem to worry too much about the ethics of God's laying booby traps for Satan. That it is a trap is made clear a few lines later when Christ replies

> Mightie Father, thou thy foes
> Justly hast in derision, and secure
> Laughst at thir vain designes . . .
>
> (V.735-737)

But God's first speech is not explicitly said to be a joke, and at the stage that it appears we have not read of any of God's jokes, or of his laughter. Even if it is a joke—God deriding Satan by seeming to accept Satan's false ideas of his independence—it is in the circumstances a particularly unpleasant one. However, there is the suspicion that rather than a joke it is a lie. Whatever it is, God is not

16. E. M. W. Tillyard, *Studies in Milton* (1951), p. 55.

speaking here as the abstract, unbiased, pure 'Word'. A personality has begun to intrude.

God would have good reasons for lying here—political reasons very similar to Satan's in his speeches to his followers; for he goes on to outline the consequences of Satan's escape—and they are so frightful that for God to admit at this point that he let Satan loose, would seem to implicate him in the evil that Satan perpetrates: it would look as if God contrived the Fall, whereas he is trying to argue that he is not responsible for it. Since he has foreknowledge, deliberately to let Satan loose would seem to suggest that he *wanted* Satan to cause the Fall. To avoid that implication, he suppresses his complicity in Satan's escape, introduces the possibilities of Manichaeism (nothing God can prescribe will keep Satan chained), and tries to shift the emphasis from the Fall to the possibility of grace for man which he brings in at the end of his speech (III.131). As long as we concentrate on his plan of producing good from evil there is the chance that we may forget his complicity in the evil: joke or lie, the effect of the passage is the same, to divert attention from what seems to be God's complicity.

That seems to be God's purpose in his speech. Are we to assume, however, that Milton was dramatizing God's motives and speech so that we can assess them? Empson remarks, 'all the characters are on trial in any civilized narrative'.[17] Are we then meant to judge the honesty and worth of God's words, just as we do Satan's? Or is Milton trying to white-wash God, deliberately trying to divert attention from the problem of foreknowledge and placing the emphasis elsewhere? But the evasions direct attention to the problem of God's complicity in the Fall, rather than divert it.

Immediately, then, there are problems about God. He goes on in his first speech to foresee what will happen. Satan is going to man,

> with purpose to assay
> If him by force he can destroy, or worse,
> By som false guile pervert; and shall pervert;
> For man will hearken to his glozing lies,
> And easily transgress the sole Command,
> Sole pledge of his obedience: So will fall
> Hee and his faithless Progenie: . . .
>
> (III.90-96)

The verb 'shall pervert' is not a simple future tense (which would have been 'will pervert', as in 'will fall') but rather emphatic future. It is as if God is ordering this to happen: again the suggestion is of his contriving the Fall, using Satan as a tool. And he once again

17. William Empson, *Milton's God* (1961), p. 94.

is not strictly honest. Beelzebub in the debate suggested that man should be attacked 'By force or suttlety' (II.358): but God by fore-knowledge knows that Satan will use subtlety, 'guile'—not force. Why does he speak as if it is uncertain whether force or guile will be used? God later even *says* what will happen; as time means nothing to God, the fact that this is said later cannot mean that he has learned more as time passed. He tells Raphael to warn Adam of his danger. The warning seems futile as God foreknows Adam will fall, and his only point in sending warning is so that he cannot be accused of not having sent any; it is an oddly petty, personal motive. Raphael's instructions from God are to tell Adam that Satan:

> Late fall'n himself from Heav'n, is plotting now
> The fall of others from like state of bliss;
> By violence, no, for that shall be withstood,
> But by deceit and lies; this let him know,
> Lest wilfully transgressing he pretend
> Surprisal, unadmonisht, unforewarnd.
>
> (V.240-245)

Why does God explicitly say that Satan will not use violence here, yet in his first speech suggests that he might?

Even more puzzling is the fact that although God makes such a point of the attack by guile that Raphael must warn Adam and Eve about, Raphael does not mention it to them. Instead, he describes Satan's use of force, in the war, to attempt to gain his ends. Further-more, as Empson states,

Raphael does once let drop, in his lengthy discourses, that Satan 'now is plotting how he may seduce' Adam (VI.901) but he never once says the practical thing which would be really likely to prevent the Fall, that Satan is known to have reached the Garden and spoken to Eve in her sleep, and will probably soon address them again in disguise. God tells Raphael that Satan has already 'disturb'd / This night the human pair', but does not tell him to tell them so. (V.226-227)[18]

Raphael's emphasis on force suggests that he listened to God's speech in Book III carefully, but not to his instructions in Book V. The result of all this is that the warning Adam and Eve get is not only inadequate, but misleading.

It is not merely that the theology of the Fall is puzzling, but Milton's treatment of it adds to the puzzle. This is further aggravated by the tone of God's speeches which, Waldock suggests, carry the 'impression of nervousness, insecurity and doubt'.[19] For, having mentioned Satan, God goes on to justify himself about Adam's Fall.

18. Empson, *Milton's God*, p. 151.
19. A. J. A. Waldock, *Paradise Lost and Its Critics* (1947), p. 103.

The fact that the justification is taking place before the Fall has occurred may dramatize God's foreknowledge, but unfortunately it also emphasizes a defensiveness; God seems touchily getting in his word before anyone begins to blame him. This reaction to him is encouraged by the personal note of the verse:

> ingrate, he had of mee
> All he could have; I made him just and right,
>
> (III.97-98)

and these hints of a Satanic egotism are developed when God gives the unfortunate explanation of the Fall.

The 'I' and 'mee' lead up to an egotistic explanation: it is all for his own 'pleasure'—and the personal tone here over-rides any abstract, metaphoric explanation. The whole speech develops into a hideous legalism in which love *from* God (as opposed to the demand of love *to* God) seems to have no place:

> Not free, what proof could they have giv'n sincere
> Of true allegiance, constant Faith or Love,
> Where only what they needs must do, appear'd,
> Not what they would? what praise could they receive?
> What pleasure I from such obedience paid,
> When Will and Reason (Reason also is choice)
> Useless and vain, of freedom both despoild,
> Made passive both, had serv'd necessitie,
> Not mee.
>
> (III.103-111)

The selfishness and egotism are brilliantly brought out by the way God returns to his 'I' again and ends resoundingly on 'mee'. And that parenthesis '(Reason also is choice)' might have come out of the small print at the bottom of a legal contract better than from the mouth of a God of love.

Why is Milton creating this sort of a God? It cannot be explained as carelessness—the verse is too finely constructed, the tone too assured. Correspondences are cunningly established: God goes on to echo the verbal rhythms of Satan's deceits—

> if I foreknew,
> Foreknowledge had no influence on their fault,
> Which had no less prov'd certain unforeknown.
>
> (III.117-119)

Broadbent has remarked that Milton was brilliantly able to deal with the complex concepts of free will, though factitiously, by a 'control of the language that designates them'.[20] But the factitious

20. *Some Graver Subject*, p. 145.

control, the verbal trickery—as after all it is—reminds us of Satan's trickery. The patterning of God's speech here is too close to Satan's,

> Surer to prosper than prosperity
> Could have assur'd us; . . .
>
> (II.39-40)

We were meant to see the falsity (and the brilliance, too) of that: having noticed verbal juggling once, we notice it again. Of course, the parallel might be merely accidental. But we still have to explain God's earlier lies. And explain, too, his statement that Adam and Eve must die, for—

> I else must change
> Thir nature, and revoke the high Decree
> Unchangeable, Eternal, . . .
>
> (III.125-127)

How can we reconcile this with God's omnipotence? Why can he not change his own mind? Are we meant to believe him here? Were the devils right in believing him subject to fate?

The conclusion to this long first speech can fairly be described as grotesque. After briefly mentioning that man shall find grace (a promise which Christ picks up and beautifully elaborates in his answer) God concludes:

> in Mercy and Justice both,
> Through Heav'n and Earth, so shall my glorie excell,
> But Mercy first and last shall brightest shine.
>
> (III.132-134)

The implication that God offers 'Mercy' and 'Justice' only for the increase of his own 'glorie' reflects ill on him—especially as he has said it himself, it is not a devilish slander. It increases the impression of his super-Satanic egotism—he tells us how good he is and, with all the blindness of egotism, tells us of the merely egotistic reasons for his goodness. Waldock remarks how ' "Mercy" comes in at the finish by an almost comical afterthought—in the very nick of time';[21] what is worse is the fact that mercy has not shone at all brightly through God's speech—nor does it through his next one. Certainly he then talks of grace, but passes on to refer to Adam's 'Treason'. The word is so inappropriate; it invokes a political context and encourages the idea of God being, as the devils said, a tyrant. It is God's own speech that prompts this association. Then God states:

21. *Paradise Lost and Its Critics*, p. 103.

> Hee with his whole posteritie must die,
> Die hee or Justice must; unless for him
> Som other able, and as willing, pay
> The rigid satisfaction, death for death.

(III.209-212)

Once again God's omnipotence is questioned. Is justice above God? Or is God lyingly suggesting it is when in fact he is omnipotent—'The organization is bigger than both of us'? It is a hideously malign justice, anyway—the Old Testament 'eye for an eye'. It is almost as if Milton were using the word in inverted commas to suggest a parody of justice. That is the impression created, too, when Hell is referred to:

> torture without end
> Still urges, and a fiery Deluge, fed
> With ever-burning Sulphur unconsum'd:
> Such place Eternal Justice had prepar'd
> For those rebellious, . . .

(I.67-70)

God's justice—satisfied if someone is punished, it does not matter who—is made deliberately unattractive; his cruelty is emphasized. After all, why cannot 'Justice' be changed, why is it better that someone should die? As Daiches notes, 'Milton here forces the argument on us *as an argument*, and if we see weaknesses in it our whole participation in the poem momentarily lessens.'[22]

God's querulousness, his nervous defensiveness, create a strange impression; his laughter (derived from *Psalms* II:4, XXXVII:13, LIX:8), which might have been symbolic of the divine happiness, comes to be something very like petty spite on Satan and on man. He has made astronomy confusing for man:

> perhaps to move
> His laughter at thir quaint Opinions wide
> Hereafter, . . .

(VIII.77-79)

The cagey 'perhaps' does not qualify the impression, enforced by the derisive satirical rhyme of 'laughter' / 'Hereafter', of malign mirth. But perhaps malign mirth is preferable to malign bad temper. Raphael explains to Adam that he was absent on the day of creation because God had commanded him and other angels to go to Hell—

> To see that none thence issu'd forth a spie
> Or enemie, while God was in his work,
> Lest hee incenst at such eruption bold,

22. Daiches, *Milton*, p. 181.

> Destruction with Creation might have mixt.
> Not that they durst without his leave attempt,
> But us he sends upon his high behests
> For state, as Sovran King, and to enure
> Our prompt obedience. . . .
>
> (VIII.233-240)

The suggestion that God cannot keep his temper is sadly damaging to the idea of him as benevolent and omnipotent. And the pointlessness of the whole guard—no one could have left Hell anyway, as the angels themselves knew—makes God seem like some madman playing with toy soldiers, or at best like Uncle Toby in *Tristram Shandy*, constructing battles in the back garden. God uses the angels to satisfy his own glory, 'for state', to satisfy his ego that they are obedient, as if—the divine paranoia—he fears they might not be.

The contrast between God the Father and God the Son is established by differences in the tone of their speeches. God's first speech ended with a strikingly staccato movement:

> The first sort by thir own suggestion fell
> Self-tempted, self-deprav'd: Man falls deceiv'd
> By th' other first: Man therefore shall find grace,
> The other none: . . .
>
> (III.129-132)

In contrast to this brusque, abrupt harshness, the Son speaks with much more gentle rhythms.

> O Father, gracious was that word which clos'd
> Thy sovran sentence, that Man should find grace:
>
> (III.144-145)

> For should Man finally be lost, should Man
> Thy creature late so lov'd, thy youngest Son
> Fall circumvented thus by fraud, though joind
> With his own folly? that be from thee farr,
> That farr be from thee, Father, . . .
>
> (III.150-154)

The word-play on 'farr'/'Father' is not like Satan's and God's, a logical trickery; rather it is a soothing, calming, almost stroking movement. The alliteration points to the gliding movement of Christ's words—'sovran sentence', 'late so lov'd', 'fall . . . by fraud'; the alliteration, assonance and repetitions evoke a gentleness that is built on to the staccato abruptness of the Father's speech.

The gentleness is built on to the abruptness. The moral law, the eternal justice is not replaced or repudiated. Rather, it is augmented

67

and subtly modified. God briefly mentions 'grace' for man, with no adornment, no amplification. Christ's reply picks up the word and develops the concept, almost like a musical variation. The dialogue is quite different from the debate in Hell. In Hell the speeches were independent blocks of rhetoric, and the final plan had been preconceived; it did not develop from any discussion. In Heaven, Christ and God do not, like the devils, offer different and incompatible schemes, nor do they argue with each other; but from the dialectic of their speeches a solution for mankind evolves. It is a solution that has not involved repudiation or rejection. When Christ suggests how terrible it would be if God destroyed man, we agree. This agreement with Christ does not imply a criticism or repudiation of what God the Father has said; indeed, God replies, 'All hast thou spoken as my thoughts are, all / As my Eternal purpose hath decreed' (III.171-172). John Peter, however, claims that,[23]

the Son's concluding sentence . . . contains a lurking admonition as to what will ensue if God should change his mind:

> So should thy goodness and thy greatness both
> Be questioned and blaspheam'd without defence.

> (III.165-166)

Such an admonition is surely not there: Christ trusts in his Father, he is not arguing with God. Christ is suggesting this as an *impossible* possibility, citing it as something inconceivable: he is saying that man is certainly saved for if God went back on his word then God's goodness and greatness would be questioned and blasphemed— and because he is God that is impossible.

Unfortunately, Peter is able to read into the speech an admonition to God because of the unfavourable impression God's first speech has made. It is too easy to see Christ as rebuking God when God is presented as so unattractive. Certainly out of the dialogue between Father and Son develops the scheme of man's redemption. God states the abstract moral law, the Son intercedes on man's behalf, and from the dialectic evolves the final synthesis satisfying both 'Justice' and 'Mercy'. But though the synthesis may finally be satisfying, the terms of the argument are less so. The happiness of the redemption does not obscure the problem of the initial harshness of God the father.

Christ's speech contrasts with God's, and pointedly so with Satan's. Satan went to seduce man alone partly from bravery, and partly from pride:

23. John Peter, *A Critique of Paradise Lost* (1960), p. 13.

                              I abroad
       Through all the Coasts of dark destruction seek
       Deliverance for us all: this enterprize
       None shall partake with me. . . .

                                        (II.463-466)

When Christ emphasizes 'I' and 'mee' it is for quite a different
purpose, and with quite a different effect.

       Behold mee then, mee for him, life for life
       I offer, on mee let thine anger fall;
       Account mee man; I for his sake will leave
       Thy bosom, and this glorie next to thee
       Freely put off, and for him lastly die
       Well pleas'd, on me let Death wreck all his rage;

                                        (III.236-241)

Christ's 'I' and 'mee' are totally without egotism or pride. They are
the note of love, of self-sacrifice, of surrender. Satan goes to destroy
man, Christ offers to die himself to save man: Satan will seek deliverance 'Through all the Coasts of dark destruction'—Christ will
seek deliverance for man by surrendering his life, not by taking life:
and his 'life for life' replies to and replaces the Father's earlier
'death for death' (III.212). Yet the success of this is limited when
Christ immediately continues:

       Though now to Death I yield, and am his due
       All that of me can die, yet that debt paid,
       Thou wilt not leave me in the loathsom grave
       His prey, nor suffer my unspotted Soul
       For ever with corruption there to dwell;

                                        (III.245-249)

To have Christ talk of his own soul as 'unspotted' is not tactful of
Milton. But more unfortunate is the way the sacrifice is immediately
reduced in significance by Christ's assurance of resurrection. The
purpose of this may well be to indicate his complete trust in God's
benevolence, but the result is a trivialization of the event. There is
no fear of death, only of a temporary period of unconsciousness.
Moreover, not only is the fact of death trivialized, the manner of
death is ignored here. It is presented as totally without the suffering,
and torture of the crucifixion, so the full force of the sacrifice is
dissipated. Milton may have felt that to present Christ fearful of
physical pain would be a breach of decorum, or that Christ as the
hero of Christian epic had to be shown as unworried by considerations
of suffering. Consequently Christ's reference to his sacrifice lacks
the power of moving us. Yet such a failure of omission is less disturbing

to the moral scheme of the poem, than Christ's description of his destruction of Death.

> But I shall rise Victorious, and subdue
> My Vanquisher, spoild of his vaunted spoil;
> Death his deaths wound shall then receive, and stoop
> Inglorious, of his mortal sting disarmd.
> I through the ample Air in Triumph high
> Shall lead Hell Captive maugre Hell, and show
> The Powers of darkness bound. Thou at the sight
> Pleas'd, out of Heaven shalt look down and smile,
> While by thee rais'd I ruin all my Foes,
> Death last, and with his Carcass glut the Grave:
>
> (III.250-259)

The archaic 'maugre' comes straight from the world of Spenser, from the 'long and tedious havoc fabl'd Knights / In Battels feignd' that is being repudiated. The same language of romance occurs again in the war in Heaven, in which Broadbent has pointed to 'terrene', 'battailous', 'weend', 'hosting', 'griding' and 'foughten'[24] (VI.78, 81, 86, 93, 329, 410). But Christ is not merely using a stray example of the vocabulary of heroic brutalism, he is acting accordingly. His description of his destruction of Death is just like Death's own behaviour. He echoes the description of Death earlier who:

> Grinnd horrible a gastly smile, to hear
> His famin should be filld, and blest his mawe
> Destind to that good hour: . . .
>
> (II.846-848)

Although it might be argued that there is an ironic appropriateness that Death shall be destroyed by his own nature, we have here not the triumphal irony of Donne's 'Death thou shalt die', but a moral confusion. Christ acts like Death: worse, God smiles like the Cheshire Cat in a way too readily reminiscent of Death's own 'gastly smile'. The poetry here has blurred the moral distinctions that should have been insisted upon.

As for the third member of the Trinity, except for a brief mention in the invocation to Book I and a description of its activities in the church in Book XII (484-530), the Holy Spirit is hardly present. Lewis is probably right in saying 'The Holy Ghost is not matter for *epic* poetry'.[25] But that is only to remind us of the difficulties of Milton's whole conception in trying to write a religious epic. His theological material is not fully suitable. After all, it does matter

---

24. *Some Graver Subject*, pp. 219-20.
25. *A Preface to Paradise Lost*, p. 85n.

theologically that the Holy Ghost is more or less forgotten. But at least that is only a sin of omission; it is the sins of commission—the not very successful portrait of God the Father—that are more disastrous. Was Milton amazingly unaware of the difficulties of his theme, amazingly naïve or amazingly confident in choosing a story in which God does not appear in the best light, and then in choosing to treat God to a large extent anthropomorphically?

To deny that there is any problem is ridiculous; but we do need to be aware that some of the problems are false ones. That we think God too harsh does not mean that Milton pictured him clumsily; Milton did not want to portray Herbert's God of love, but rather a God who demanded a strict discipline of obedience. On the other hand, to say that any of our objections to his God are wrong because God is right always and that that is a *donnée* of the poem, would also seem mistaken. If that were so, there would be no point to Milton's poem, no point to his attempt to 'justifie the wayes of God to men'. It is because God's ways are obscure, because his excessive brightness appears dark, that a justification is not pointless.

The justification involves presenting not only what God the Father says, but also what the Son says, and what evolves from their dialogue; not only what God in his anger declares, but what in his love he does. Milton's God is to be seen not merely in the speeches of the Father, but also in the speeches of Christ, and in the act of Christ's intercession, in the act of the creation and of the redemption. God's anger, wrath and arbitrary legalism are only one aspect. The final emphasis rests on the action of producing good out of evil, on the celestial cycle. The evil of the fall of the Angels produces the creation; the evil of the fall of man produces the redemption.

Even here problems still remain. Even if we see God the Father's harshness subsumed into the celestial cycle of good out of evil, we still have uanswerable questions about the origins of evil. Grierson observed of the angels' fall that 'if the third part of a school or college or nation broke into rebellion we should be driven, or strongly disposed, to suspect some mismanagement by the supreme powers'.[26] Empson indeed would argue that Milton intends to drive us to such suspicions, intends us to reconsider God. It may seem an extreme view of the poem: but the alternative makes things no easier. Roy Daniells has expressed that position well: 'when Milton, who has undertaken to justify the ways of God to men, brings us into the presence of a God who is demanding "true allegiance, constant Faith or love" from Adam, because he has created him, we are in the presence of a quite inexplicable absolute. Rebellion

26. H. J. C. Grierson, *Milton and Wordsworth: Poets and Prophets* (1937), p. 116.

against such a God seems equally irrational. The origins of evil in Satan are as mysterious as the origins of good in his maker.'[27]

We can react to the mysterious in different ways; we can argue that the mysterious is unknowable, and accept God's goodness by a leap of faith; or we can grope towards an understanding and try to interpret upon the basis of what evidence we have. Milton does not leap over the problems and disregard them. Far from being a monument to dead ideas, in Raleigh's phrase, *Paradise Lost* is urgently and actively concerned with immediate problems. Milton is not building a wall to shut out our questions, or a monument to celebrate a static acceptance. The dialectic of the debate in Heaven deliberately involves us as readers. We are not simply watching theological pictures, but are being involved in a consideration of the issues of justice, forgiveness, obedience. Significantly, Milton's Arianism is an issue of his *De Doctrina Christiana* but not of *Paradise Lost*; *Paradise Lost* is not concerned with the merely theological. We do not need to believe in Milton's God—or in any god—to appreciate it; the issues of the poem are of all time. Why is there suffering? How did evil originate? Why do ideal societies fail? What is justice? How can things be improved? These questions are as relevant in an H-bomb age as they were after the Civil War. By the dialectic of the Father and Son—and by the action of the whole poem—Milton provokes us to think deeply about the moral issues of justice-obedience-suffering that cluster round the Fall, just as by the presentation of Satan he forced us to question heroism. Milton is concerned to arouse our questioning and meditating, not our placid acceptance. God is significantly presented by the Son-Father dialectic, not by an abstract, static force.

And so we are involved in the questioning of what is heroism, what is justice, why is there evil in the world? But our questioning does not stop there; we go on to ask why is there evil in Heaven, why did Satan *become* corrupt, why is God God? If we follow through with Milton's Protestant questioning we soon end like the devils:

> Of good and evil much they argu'd then,
> Of happiness and final misery,
> Passion and Apathie, and glory and shame,
> Vain wisdom all, and false Philosophie:
>
> (II.562-565)

Where is the line to be drawn, and who is to draw it? When we become involved in questioning God's goodness and justice have we been led to that by a flaw in the poem's intellectual structure, by Milton's demanding a leap of faith, putting up a barrier, when the questions

27. Roy Daniells, *Milton, Mannerism and Baroque* (1963), p. 78.

get too difficult? He too facilely describes the devils' questioning as vain and false—which might indicate an anti-intellectual blocking of certain sorts of questions. Yet alternatively, have we perhaps been led to where Milton wants us to be? For Empson, 'the poem is wonderful because it is an awful warning not against eating the apple but against worshipping that God'.

The war in Heaven has never had many champions amongst Milton's readers. Yet it was an essential part of Milton's conception. If he was going to outdo classical, pagan epic he had the alternatives of writing a bigger and better version of the classical, of or writing something morally superior to the classical. He chose to do both; he repudiates classical heroism and offers the morally superior 'patience and heroic martyrdom'; but he does not repudiate it before showing that he can anyway write in the classical conventions: so, in the war, expanded from the brief reference in *Revelations* XII, the fallen angels surpass classical heroes' physical strength by throwing mountains.

The result becomes ridiculous—and this is Milton's intention; he is showing he can create a bigger and better war than any classical writer, and by expanding it to such dimensions, he is able to deride the whole convention of military grandeur in the pagan epic. It becomes a type of all the wars of history, only worse: 'Warr seemd a civil Game / To this uproar' (VI.667-668). John Peter has argued that as the wounds cannot be fatal the reader can hardly get involved in the battle;[28] it is a comment Milton might have delighted in: fallen man needs to see murder and carnage to get excited! Milton avoids pandering to that sort of taste—and by avoiding that, shows how dull war is unless there are lots of deaths. And the fact that the angels cannot be killed emphasizes a further feature of the war— its inconclusiveness:

> in perpetual fight they needs must last
> Endless, and no solution will be found:
> Warr wearied hath performd what Warr can do,
>
> (VI.693-695)

The pointlessness of war, the way in which it will continue uselessly, indefinitely, is Milton's salutary point.

There is the danger, of course, that the poem itself will become as dull as the material being described—a danger Milton does not fully avoid. Waldock has pointed to what he felt was a failing of this episode:

28. *A Critique of Paradise Lost*, p. 76.

73

For much of the time Milton seems unhappy, straining for his effects. There is expense of effort for no proportionate result.

> So under fierie Cope together rushd
> Both Battels main, with ruinous assault
> And inextinguishable rage: . . . (VI.215)

Does this cause a flutter? One's ears become insensitive to the operative words: rage, ruin, dreadful, amazement, destruction, horrid, hideous, confusion. The imagery is grandiose, conventional, unrealized . . .[29]

Of course the imagery is 'conventional' because Milton is satirizing the conventional attitudes. And the 'expense of effort for no proportionate effect' is an exact imaging in the verse of the inconclusive heroic activities of the war. Milton is not 'straining for his effects' and failing to achieve them here: his effects are deliberately of insensitive grandiosity. The 'conventional' is parodied. Waldock's accusation that it is unrealized, however, qualifies our enthusiasm for the book; we might wonder if Milton's satiric intentions succeed, or as Broadbent argues, backfire. If we argue that the war is intentionally comic, we must admit that it has been too easy for readers from Voltaire to Waldock to fail to realize that this was deliberate.

The most stimulating reading of the war is by Arnold Stein.[30] He argues that if we try to read it as a realistic war we cannot escape Dr Johnson's objection:

The confusion of spirit and matter which pervades the whole narration of the war of heaven fills it with incongruity; and the book, in which it is related, is, I believe, the favourite of children, and gradually neglected as knowledge is increased.[31]

Stein suggests a metaphorical reading. Raphael told Adam he would describe 'what surmounts the reach / Of human sense . . . / By lik'ning spiritual to corporeal forms, / As may express them best' (V.571-574) —and Stein argues that by a metaphorical reading what to Johnson had seemed childish incongruity, is seen as 'controlled confusion, the dramatic working out of what Satan ignorantly set in motion'.[32] The confusion of spirit and matter is not incompetent realism, but meaningful metaphor. 'The invention of artillery is an attempt to usurp ultimate moral might by means of matter . . . It is setting matter against spirit by means of mind.'[33] The confusion is Satan's own.

29. *Paradise Lost and Its Critics*, p. 111.
30. Arnold Stein, *Answerable Style* (1953), pp. 17-37.
31. *Lives of the Poets* (World's Classics edn, 1952) I, p. 128.
32. *Answerable Style*, p. 31.
33. Stein, *Answerable Style*, p. 37.

The dominant mood of the war is, Stein argues, 'a kind of great scherzo, like some of Beethoven's—with more than human laughter, too elevated, and comprehensive, and reverberating not to be terribly funny'.[34] And so we see God's laughter deriding Satan, and we see Satan conducting his campaign by ridicule too. He uses the cannon as much for puns as for armaments, ironically giving the order to fire in seeming terms of peace. After the first fusillade, he comments 'in derision':

> O Friends, why come not on these Victors proud?
> Erewhile they fierce were coming, and when wee
> To entertain them fair with open Front
> And Brest (what could we more?) propounded terms
> Of composition, straight they chang'd thir minds,
> Flew off, and into strange vagaries fell,
> As they would dance, . . .
>
> (VI.609-615)

Addison strongly objected to this passage: 'the most exceptionable in the whole poem, as being nothing else but a string of puns, and those too very indifferent'. [35] Yet he did recognize the comic intention of the episode. And the verbal derision of the punning is succeeded by the physical insult and mockery in Satan's comment on the angels' 'dance'; the laughter at the punning is swelled by laughter at the slapstick action. The climax of the battle is a passage of grotesque comedy—

> . . . Hills amid the Air encounterd Hills
> Hurld to and fro with jaculation dire,
> That under ground they fought in dismal shade:
>
> (VI.664-666)

Waldock said 'one would like to think that even Milton giggled'[36] at this; but he did not suspect that Milton intended it as comedy—one of the earliest black comedies.

There are, unfortunately, moral confusions in the idea of the war. If war is evil, why does God participate in it? He has no need to—he could just have thrown out the fallen angels at once; indeed, instead of doing that, he even limits the good angels' power. Moreover, he tells Michael to defeat the devils—'drive them out' (VI.52)—and then after limiting Michael's power repeats (as Peter notes[37]) the same order verbatim to Christ (VI. 715). The whole episode

34. *Answerable Style*, p. 28.
35. Joseph Addison, *The Spectator*, No. 279.
36. *Paradise Lost and Its Critics*, p. 112.
37. *A Critique of Paradise Lost*, p. 79.

looks like a put-up job for Christ—the sort of favouritism that made Satan rebel in the first place.

Christ's defeat of the fallen angels is the original defeat of Satan, but it is also an image of the later defeat of him when Christ harrows Hell after the crucifixion,[38] and of the final defeat of evil to come with the last judgement. The war has imaged the universal struggle of evil against good, chaos against creation—but Christ's victory images the ultimate final victory. And Christ defeats evil not by cannon, hill-throwing or any physical assault, but by his 'Godly' appearance. The chariot of wrath is fully metaphorical in a way that the metaphoric ridicule of the war is not. In the war the details of blows, wounds, injuries were described in detail, because the war was an archetype of earthly war. Christ's defeat of the fallen angels has none of this restricting earthly detail; it is something quite dissimilar, quite transcendent.

38. *See* Louis L. Martz, *The Paradise Within* (1964), p. 124 for the significance of the three-day struggle.

CHAPTER IV

Earth

The creation of Earth is God's triumph and the mark of his great goodness in making it so wonderful—'Earth now / Seemd like to Heav'n, a seat where Gods might dwell, / Or wander with delight' (VII.328-330). The pinnacles of creation are mankind, and the garden of Paradise. The account of the creation of Adam in Book VII is rather perfunctory but it is amplified, as in *Genesis* (cf. I.26-28, II.5-25) by a second account. Adam tells Raphael how his immediate reaction, after finding he could name all he saw, was to ask:

> how came I thus, how here?
> Not of my self; by some great Maker then,
> In goodness and in power præeminent;
>
> (VIII.277-279)

This spontaneous recognition of a creator is the answer to Satan's jibes at Abdiel:

> who saw
> When this creation was? rememberst thou
> Thy making, while the Maker gave thee being?
> We know no time when we were not as now;
> Know none before us, self-begot, self-rais'd
> By our own quick'ning power, . . .
>
> (V.856-861)

Satan's argument is not (as Lewis claims[1]) stupid; though it is not conclusive proof, it cannot be disproved by Abdiel. What *is* wrong is that Satan lacks faith, love of God, spontaneous obedience—all of which we find demonstrated in Adam's first reactions.

Adam is born on Earth and then taken to the garden of Eden. As the pinnacle of creation, Eden is appropriately a mountain; the early Christian Fathers had made it a mountain so that it was high above winds, storms and extremes of heat and cold.[2] And the fact

---

1. C. S. Lewis, *A Preface to Paradise Lost* (1942), pp. 95-6.
2. *See* Grant McColley, *Paradise Lost* (Chicago, 1940), pp. 142-3.

that it is a mountain enforces the metaphorical pattern of rising and falling. Adam is taken upwards to the goodness of Eden; after the Fall, Adam and Eve are driven from Eden 'down the Cliff as fast / To the subjected Plain' (XII.639-640), metaphorically re-enacting the Fall. And we first see Paradise from the position of fallen readers, at the foot of the mountain, and through Satan's eyes. We approach it from outside, and below.

It is resistant to our access. It seems protected, yet as there is no evil in the world yet, what against? Satan's evil and energy are such that ordinary protection is useless: the 'hairie sides / With thicket overgrown, grottesque and wild, / Access deni'd' (IV.135-137)—but that was no discouragement.

> Due entrance he disdaind, and in contempt
> At one slight bound high overleap'd all bound
> Of Hill or highest Wall, . . .
>
> (IV.180-182)

His contempt is caught in that finely contemptuous pun on 'bound'. But if he can be so easily contemptuous of Eden's defences, why is it not better protected? The Fall so often seems inevitable; and the prefiguring of it, the ironic prolepses, encourage that suggestion.

> God had thrown
> That Mountain as his Garden mould high rais'd
> Upon the rapid current, . . .
>
> (IV.225-227)

we are told of Paradise. It reminds us of the mountains thrown in the war—as if it is one flung down to Earth: indeed creation is a result of the evil of the war. But if it has been 'thrown' once, it can be moved again easily—as it is after the Fall (XI.829ff.). From its first mention, then, the mount of Paradise is shown as vulnerable. The Fall is suggested, too, in the description of the river of Paradise; after leaving the garden it,

> . . . now divided into four main Streams
> Runs diverse, wandring many a famous Realm
>
> (IV.233-234)

The four rivers parallel with a tragic irony the four rivers of Hell; the 'wandring' suggests fallen man—the 'wandring steps' of Adam and Eve leaving Paradise after the Fall; and Hell is suggested further by 'the nether Flood' (line 231) which the united rills of Paradise 'fell' to meet—just as Adam and Eve will fall to meet the Hellish rivers. Man will leave Paradise and wander, like the divided rivers, through a fallen world of famous realms—the fallen world already imaged in Hell.

In Paradise, the rivers are a pattern of perfect order, of variety in unity.

> Southward through *Eden* went a River large,
> Nor chang'd his course, but through the shaggie hill
> Passd underneath ingulft, for God had thrown
> That Mountain as his Garden mould high rais'd
> Upon the rapid current, which through veins
> Of porous Earth with kindly thirst up drawn,
> Rose a fresh Fountain, and with many a rill
> Waterd the Garden; thence united fell
> Down the steep glade, and met the nether Flood,
> Which from his darksom passage now appears,
>
> (IV.223-232)

The waters flow in a perfect symmetry; they feed the garden below, above and within (the Earth is 'porous'); and the divided waters after flowing separately, re-unite.

The whole irrigation system is described in language suggestive of human thirst and drinking; the geological 'veins' suggest biological ones; the Earth's 'thirst' is like man's, not in its mechanics (this thirst is satisfied intravenously not orally) but in the general principle and process. Already we have seen the side of the mountains as 'hairie' and 'shaggie', the valley has a 'flourie lap', the waters are 'murmuring'. The anthropomorphic suggestions mark nature's closeness to prelapsarian man—a closeness in function that creates a closeness of sympathy. The thirst, hence, is 'kindly'—and the pun emphasizes Milton's idea of unfallen Eden: 'kindly' means 'benevolent' and also 'natural'. Because the thirst is natural, part of a natural process, it is also benevolent; in the unfallen world nature *is* benevolent.

The garden that is being watered is a complex creation of all natural and artistic features—of mineral perfection, jewels and gems, as well as of floral perfection; of literary tradition and visual image; of picture and evocation; of traditional symbol and personal realization. Milton intends

> to tell how, if Art could tell,
> How from that Saphire Fount the crisped Brooks,
> Rouling on Orient Pearl and sands of Gold,
> With mazie error under pendant shades
> Ran Nectar, visiting each plant, and fed
> Flowrs worthy of Paradise which not nice Art
> In Beds and curious Knots, but Nature boon
> Pourd forth profuse on Hill and Dale and Plain,

Both where the morning Sun first warmly smote
The open field, and where the unpierc't shade
Imbrownd the noontide Bowrs: Thus was this place,
A happy rural seat of various view;
Groves whose rich Trees wept odorous Gumms and Baum,
Others whose fruit burnisht with Golden Rinde
Hung amiable, *Hesperian* Fables true,
If true, here only, and of delicious taste:

(IV.236-251)

The brooks are described in terms of art, in the aureate diction of
Chaucer, Dunbar and Spenser. Leavis complained about 'the
laboured, pedantic artifice of the diction' in 'Saphire', 'Orient Pearl',
'sands of Gold', saying that they 'convey no doubt a vague sense of
opulence, but this is not what we mean by "sensuous richness"'.[3]
Clearly they do not offer a Keatsian sensuous richness, nor were
they meant to; they are creating a jewelled and ornate Paradise,
deliberately in terms of 'Art', self-consciously 'artificial'—and the
traditional vocabulary is used to insist on this traditional, formal
perfection; just as the '*Hesperian* Fables' insist on the literary ante-
cedents (or descendants?) of this garden. It is only one aspect of
Paradise. Milton goes on to complement the artistic aspect with the
sensuous naturalness—the pastoral as opposed to the courtly—with
the flowers 'pourd forth profuse'. In its reduplicative alliterative
pattern, the phrase suggests teeming fertility. The profusion is a
fertility of procreation, suggestive of human birth—'the flowrie lap /
Of som irriguous Valley'—and this anthropomorphism is brought
out further in the trees that 'weep' and in the fruit hanging 'amiable'
with a 'Golden Rinde'. With rind, Milton is playing on the now
obsolete sense of a skin not just of a fruit but of an animal—as
leviathan's 'Rinde' (I.206). Vegetable is like animal in this unity of
Paradise; and 'burnisht with Golden Rinde' reminds us of the
'vegetable Gold' of the fruit of the Tree of Life where mineral and
organic are in unity. The gold is vegetable and growing—and
Milton creates this fusion by a further ambiguity: 'burnisht' means
polished bright—as if the fruit is indeed gold that shines—but it also
meant to grow plump or stout. ('My thoughts began to burnish,
sprout, and swell' Herbert wrote in 'Jordan II'.) So we have a fine
synthesis of the animal (rind), the vegetable (the fruit swelling) and
the mineral (the gold shining). The trees are 'rich' in possessing
such financial wealth of golden fruit; but they are rich, too, with sap,
with gum, with organic life as well as mineral wealth. And the
fruit, too, is rich to taste—an obvious richness that Milton transfers
to the trees themselves, as well as pointing to in their 'delicious taste'.

3. F. R. Leavis, *Revaluation* (1936), pp. 49-50.

Taste, together with the tactile suggestions of the fruit being polished, combine with the visual beauty and the scents of the 'odorous' gums and balm to establish a complete sensuous richness—'All Trees of noblest kind for sight, smell, taste' (IV.217), while the sound of the verse itself, the art evoking the nature, provides the fifth sense.

Paradise is rich, but it is also a world of simplicity; the beauty is there in the simple alternation of sun and shade, open meadow and enclosed bower. It is a nature that is ordered, too—simple but planned.

> Betwixt them Lawns or level Downs, and Flocks
> Grazing the tender herb, were interpos'd,
> Or palmie hillock, or the flowrie lap
> Of som irriguous Valley spred her store,
> Flowrs of all hue, and without Thorn the Rose:
> Another side, umbrageous Grots and Caves
>
> (IV.252-257)

Nature is there for the good of man, so we see flocks grazing as if they were domestic—though before the Fall there was no need to domesticate them, they were naturally friendly and obedient. Nature is for man's service and so supplies him—'spred her store'. This is not a Romantic nature rampaging wild for its own sake, expressing itself as nature; nature here serves man. This service is expressed in the order; 'interpos'd' suggests that God's hand has arranged the whole garden like a three-dimensional painting—as 'Lantskip' (IV.153) has already suggested. It is arranged and ordered by God, by an art far superior to man's 'nice Art', for man's delight.

And because it is not wild but ordered, not an excess of growth but a productive fecundity for man's use, the suggestions of a country-house are appropriate: 'Thus was this place, / A happy rural seat of various view.' It is like an idealized country mansion, not in any architectural construction, obviously, but like it in the landscaped grounds and in the rural domestic security and in the contentment evoked—a contrast to the wild savages discovered by Columbus (IX.1115) and to the industrial urban society of Hell. God calls Eden to Adam 'Thy Mansion' and 'thy seat' (VIII.296, 299), insisting on these associations appropriate for Adam's lordly dignity, and the whole place is like a landscaped estate 'with goodliest Trees / Planted, with Walks and Bowers' (VIII.304-305). The trees did not just grow, as Satan claimed *he* did, but God 'planted' them.

The formal implications of the country 'seat' are qualified in Book IV by the complete simplicity, by the innocence of emotion, evoked by 'happie'. It is a simplicity forming a fine alliance with the formal pomp of 'rural seat'. It is an innocence that is brought out again with simplicity in the seeming afterthought to the general description of the flowers, in the particularization of detail tagged on with a seeming naïvety of manner that catches the naïve innocence; 'Flowrs of all hue, and without Thorn the Rose'.

We might, however, wonder in this idyllic Eden why trees should weep, why 'baum', with its connotations of embalming the dead, should be wept. Even in this peaceful innocence the Fall is being foreshadowed, the beautiful fruit of the forbidden tree is hinted at by these trees, the results of eating the fruit are foreshadowed in the hint of death. When the rose is mentioned, we are reminded that there will be thorns, and we are told that the brooks run 'With mazie error under pendant shades'—the deceitful maze and the sinful error, the shades not fallen but hanging suspended, ready to fall.

The innocence is so vulnerable; the passage goes on to a reference to Proserpin being gathered to the underworld by Dis which suggests (but with no explicit comparison being made) how Eve will be gathered by Satan (IV.268ff.). The Fall and loss of innocence and the arrival of death are just hinted at in the first description of Paradise. It is something that gives the beauty an added poignancy, a fragility, something that underlines its worth, its rarity, by reminding us how it will be lost for ever. After all, we are seeing Eden through Satan's eyes—'the Fiend / Saw undelighted all delight' (IV.285-286). The Devil has already entered Paradise when we see it; the Fall is already impending. We never do—and never could— see innocence unimpinged on by evil. The very first time Eden was mentioned in the poem (as Daiches points out[4]) it was in connection with the word loss—'with loss of *Eden*' (I.4).

To consider any aspect of *Paradise Lost* is to realize the huge difficulties of Milton's task. God was problem enough—yet so were Adam and Eve. How could they be interesting before the Fall, when they were innocent, uncorrupt, when they did not have to toil, had no need to invent things, had only a limited range of emotions—no anger, despair, envy, aggression and so on?

Milton's presentation of their relationship as fully sexual has often been admired for its unpuritanicalness, and justly. But sex was one of the few activities and emotions he could show Adam and Eve engaged in: and distinguished from postlapsarian sex, he is able to make important points about the results of the Fall. So unfallen sexuality is emphasized, Eve's nakedness drawn attention to:

> Shee as a veil down to the slender waist
> Her unadorned golden tresses wore
> Dissheveld, but in wanton ringlets wav'd

4. David Daiches, 'The Opening of "Paradise Lost" ' in Frank Kermode (ed.), *The Living Milton* (1960), p. 59.

As the Vine curls her tendrils, which impli'd
Subjection, but requir'd with gentle sway,
And by her yielded, by him best receiv'd,
Yielded with coy submission, modest pride,
And sweet reluctant amorous delay.
Nor those mysterious parts were then conceal'd,
Then was not guiltie shame, dishonest shame
Of Natures works: honor dishonorable,
Sin-bred, how have ye troubl'd all mankind
With shews instead, mere shews of seeming pure,
And banisht from mans life his happiest life,
Simplicitie and spotless innocence.

(IV.304-318)

Naked, but with her hair half covering her, Eve is presented more erotically than if she were unveiled. Milton presents not a simply naked Eve, but an Eve whose nakedness is used to suggest sexuality: there is something of the art of the striptease—her veiling hair, her 'sweet reluctant amorous delay' to arouse sexual interest. And the delight of unfallen sex is heightened by the polemical intrusion of the narrative voice—with 'guiltie shame' contrasted directly against 'spotless innocence'. The despair of the narrative voice, here, heightens the sense of the marvellousness of what has been lost. And it is worth emphasizing that Milton presents sex as an enjoyment in its own right, not merely as the mechanics of procreation: the angels make love, but do not breed. Adam and Eve make love, too, because they enjoy it: Milton is not at all 'puritanical' here.

According to a theory of human primary drives held by some psychologists, man has three (some claim four) basic needs for survival and perpetuation of the species—hunger, thirst, sex, and, as the possible fourth, a stimulation drive, involving a need to explore, to manipulate things, a need for stimulation. It is these four activities that provide Milton with the occupations of his primary couple: secondary drives, dependent on social environment and on learning, develop after the Fall. In addition he gives them another activity—prayer to God. The work that they do can be seen as a fulfilment of the stimulation drive, but it is also a manifestation of their worship and love of God: the Puritan emphasis on the good of work, that Milton shows, is based on the assumption that work is ultimately for God's glory; the Devil finds work for idle hands.

Just as prelapsarian sex differs from fallen sex (in being without guilt and shame), so hunger and thirst are different before the Fall. In Eden Adam and Eve do not have to toil for their food, there is never anything to prevent them from being satisfied, and Milton presents these drives not in terms of the effort involved in satisfying them, nor in terms of being unsatisfied, but in a celebration of the end-process of the preparation and consuming of food and drink. In contrast is the agony of the devils 'parcht with scalding thirst and hunger fierce' (X.556).

As with sex (VIII.615ff.), Milton insists on the sharing of hunger and thirst with the angels. When Raphael joins Adam and Eve for dinner and Milton drifts once more into his polemical style and refutes (as Lewis points out[5]) Aquinas' claim that angels were incorporeal and did not eat he shows Raphael eating 'with keen dispatch / Of real hunger, and concoctive heat / To transubstantiate' (V.436-438). The scientific jargon indicates that Milton believed this account to be true; but the belief is not merely quaint angelology. Milton insists on the way in which angels share with man's activities like sex, hunger and thirst since this indicates man's closeness to the angels; he is below them on the Chain of Being—but if the angels are similarly corporeal as man, though more refined, man may become refined enough to be like them. They are not totally different in kind. Raphael goes on shortly afterwards to expound (V.470ff.) the possibility of man's becoming like the angels. With the Fall, however, man became more like the beasts.

Not only is man like the angels, his activities of sex, eating and drinking are activities of the universe—again indicating his closeness to the whole universe, suggesting man as microcosm. The whole process of the universe is described in a metaphor of eating and digesting—'whatever was created, needs / To be sustain and fed' (V.414ff.). Adam is seen looking at a sunset that is described in terms of human sexuality:

> in the dore he sat
> Of his cool Bowre, while now the mounted Sun
> Shot down direct his fervid Rays, to warme
> Earths inmost womb, more warmth than *Adam* needs:
> And *Eve* within, due at her hour prepar'd
> For dinner savourie fruits, of taste to please
> True appetite, and not disrelish thirst
> Of nectarous draughts between, from milkie stream,
> Berrie or Grape: . . .
>
> (V.299-307)

The sun is 'mounted', his rays are phallic, ejaculating into Earth's womb. Human sex is like the universe, just as human eating is like the universe—and like the gods' too; the milkie stream and nectarous draughts evoke the promised land flowing with milk and honey shown to Moses; but nectar is also the 'drink of Gods' (IX.838) indicating the splendour of Eden. It is a very beautiful and richly

5. *A Preface to Paradise Lost*, p. 105ff.

complex passage. Eating here (as V.414ff.) becomes another image of order and harmony; the sun with regularity 'at Even / Sups with the Ocean' (V.425-426) and here Eve, too, with equivalent regularity 'due at her hour' gets dinner.

There is an order of time—everything happening at its proper hour—and there is also an order of hierarchy; in the universe 'The grosser feeds the purer' (V.416); here it is charmingly demonstrated in the picture of woman, inferior to man (in the seventeenth-century view), feeding him. The hierarchy is humanized with the delightful picture of Eve preparing the meal inside while Adam sits in his doorway—like any village couple on a summer's evening. It is domestic touches like this that make the picture of Adam and Eve so successful.

They are domestic, and indeed they are often presented as thoroughly simple and primitive. In our first meeting with them we see them pick fruit:

> The savourie pulp they chew, and in the rinde
> Still as they thirsted scoop the brimming stream;

> (IV.335-336)

The shells they drink from beautifully evoke them as simple, unfallen and so without tools: above all natural. 'Chew' is appropriately and marvellously direct and unperiphrastic. But, as Lewis emphasized, they are not naked savages.[6] They have an ambassadorial dignity when Raphael is entertained.

> Mean while at Table *Eve*
> Ministerd naked, and thir flowing cups
> With pleasant liquors crownd: . . .

> (V.443-445)

The flowing cups in this context evoke goblets; the liquors imply, but are tactfully unspecific, wines and liqueurs befitting the occasion. With great brilliance Milton has created a natural dignity, a 'naked Majestie' (IV.290), a 'naked Glorie' (IX.1115). They are majestic and glorious because they are naked, because their full perfections are unconcealed; and because, as their nakedness testifies, they are unfallen, uncorrupted; but the phrase also suggests that their majesty and glory are naked, unobscured, unsmeared; we see pure, unconcealed majesty and glory. Their nakedness insists on their primitiveness, their foods, for instance, are always simple; but the glory and 'majestie' insist on their regality. They are simultaneously simpler and nobler than fallen man. Perhaps, the pastoral suggests,

6. *A Preface to Paradise Lost*, Chapter XVI.

they are nobler because they are simpler. The ceremony of Hell is the obvious contrast.

Unfallen man's need for stimulation is satisfied by work:

> Man hath his daily work of body or mind
> Appointed, which declares his Dignitie,
> And the regard of Heav'n on all his ways;
> While other Animals unactive range,
> And of thir doings God takes no account.
>
> (IV.618-622)

The animals are content to subsist, but man has other drives. Milton makes them two-fold—both physical and mental. The mental work we see in the amount of time Adam and Eve spend in learning; Adam inquires of things from Raphael, Eve asks Adam why the stars shine (IV.657ff.). The time between our first sight of the couple, in Book IV, till the events leading up to the Fall in Book IX, is spent mainly in Adam's learning. Milton's problem of what to give the unfallen couple to do is to some extent economically solved: they need to be given information, and the time spent in giving them this will occupy them before the Fall, and give the reader the sense of time passing, and of seeing Adam and Eve; at the same time Raphael's narrative gives the reader the necessary background to the whole situation—the rebellion, war and creation. Thus we are shown Adam engaged in one of his prime activities; at his first appearance he was described as 'For *contemplation* hee and valour formd' (IV.297, my italics), reminding us, as Samuel notes 'of the end which Plato set as man's chief good'.[7] Hence we see him learning from Raphael not only history, but also psychology, angelology and astronomy. Knowledge is something valuable—which makes the serpent's offer of 'wisdome' and 'knowledge' so appealing to Eve.

The 'daily work of body' is shown in the gardening. It is not hard labour, although as Adam says to Eve with a beautifully simple human lover's compliment, even 'were it toilsom, yet with thee were sweet' (IV.439). The compliment suggests that not only is the gardening pleasant, sufficiently stimulating to keep them happy, but just to be with each other is bliss too: the combination is idyllic. It is an idyllic world of pastoral, but the accurately technical language—'Lop overgrown, or prune, or prop, or bind' (IX.210)—invokes a naturalism that creates the sense of a genuine activity.

It is an important symbolic activity, too. As with their frequent hymns, it shows Adam and Eve proclaiming in word and deed the glory of God. It shows, also, their position on the Chain of Being—distinguishing them from the animals who do not work, showing

---

7. Irene Samuel, *Plato and Milton* (1947), p. 110.

their superiority to the nature that they control in their pruning, binding and lopping. The gardening is an enactment of this hierarchical scheme. They tend where,

> . . . Fruit-trees overwoodie reach'd too farr
> Thir pamperd boughs, and needed hands to check
> Fruitless imbraces: or they led the Vine
> To wed her Elm; . . .
>
> (V.213-216)

Their control is a kindly one—a closeness and helpfulness. To enforce the closeness, Eve herself is compared to the vine—her hair 'in wanton ringlets wav'd / As the Vine curls her tendrils' (IV.306-307). While just as they kindly help nature, nature responds with a similar kindness, showing the unity in Eden. When they are asleep in their bower 'on thir naked limbs the flowrie roof / Showrd Roses, which the Morn repaird' (IV.772-773), the nightingale sings to them, and in the day-time the animals play before them to entertain them (IV.340ff.). The work and the response it provokes are not a toil but a celebration of nature's richness and God's goodness.

Adam and Eve's own union is expressed by the simplest of phrases, as Charles Williams showed.[8] When we first see them, 'So hand in hand they passd' (IV.321), the phrase is an image of their unity. It becomes a sort of icon: 'Thus talking hand in hand alone they passd / On to thir blissful Bower' (IV.689-690) and Milton offers variants such as 'into thir inmost bower / Handed they went' (IV.738-9). Our final picture of them, united again at the end, is when they leave Eden 'hand in hand' (XII.648), and the re-establishment of their closeness to God after the alienation of the Fall is imaged when Michael leads them from the garden—'In either hand the hastning Angel caught / Our lingring Parents' (XII.637-638).

The maintenance of the perfect union of Adam and Eve depends upon observation of their proper relationship to each other. They are both 'Godlike erect' though,

> Not equal, as thir sex not equal seemd;
> For contemplation hee and valour formd,
> For softness shee and sweet attractive Grace,
> Hee for God only, shee for God in him:
>
> (IV.296-299)

Their individual beauties are due to this inequality. He is manly, 'His fair large Front and Eye sublime declar'd / Absolute rule' (IV.300-301), whereas she is soft and submissive, and her hair curling

---

8. Charles Williams, introduction to *The English Poems of Milton* (World's Classics edn, 1940), p. xix.

like the vine 'impli'd / Subjection, but requir'd with gentle sway' (IV.307-308). The scheme is hierarchical, but it is not, and Milton emphasizes this, authoritarian. Eve must be treated with gentleness, with courtesy, just as she must accept Adam's gentle authority with submission. Too often passages like these have been read as examples of Milton's egotism, misogyny or arrogance; but they are commonplaces, examples of 'the deepest and most impersonal feelings of the time';[9] happiness and perfect union will exist for Adam and Eve as long as Eve accepts that she is the inferior.

The gardening and cooking, eating and drinking and love making, even the hymns to God and the love poetry and dialogues on astronomy, cannot give Adam and Eve much personality; they remain different from Satan in that respect. And Milton's intention was to present them in general terms; they will develop personal traits, but it is their general nature that is important. Because Adam and Eve are the founders of the human race, the human genus, they must be described in general enough terms so that what is said of them could apply to all ensuing individuals. ' "The business of a poet," said Imlac, "is to examine, not the individual, but the species" ', Dr Johnson wrote in Chapter X of *Rasselas* (1759). Pre-Romantic poetry dealt with the general, rather than with the specific detail and concrete imagery in favour with twentieth-century critics; much of the difficulty the twentieth-century reader finds with the portrayal of Adam and Eve is due to this change in critical taste (preferring the detail to the general), and to a failure to realize that Milton *had* to present his couple as general. To give them too distinct character traits would in fact be to limit them. The painter Sir Joshua Reynolds commented in 1778 on Milton's method—understanding its principles and almost envious of its advantages:

A great part of the beauty of the celebrated description of Eve in Milton's *Paradise Lost* consists in using only general indistinct expressions, every reader making out the detail according to his own particular imagination,—his own idea of beauty, grace, expression, dignity or loveliness: but a painter, when he represents Eve on a canvas, is obliged to give a determined form, and his own idea of beauty distinctly expressed.[10]

Yet it is a generality kept within firm control: Milton never generalizes them out of existence. Sir Thomas Browne saw in the temptation of the man by the woman 'the seduction of the rational and higher parts by the inferior and feminine faculties'.[11] Though we see that

9. *See* St Paul, *Ephesians* V:22; B. Rajan, *Paradise Lost and the Seventeenth Century Reader* (1947), p. 66 *and* Helen Gardner, *A Reading of Paradise Lost* (1965), pp. 81-4.
10. Sir Joshua Reynolds, *Discourses on Art*, 8 (Collier paperback edn, 1961), p. 145.
11. *See* Rajan, *Paradise Lost and the Seventeenth Century Reader*, p. 67.

'seduction' occurring when Adam tells Raphael how his love for Eve degrades his reason (VIII.546ff.), Milton never allegorizes the story into such abstractions. To have done so might have been a temptation; but Milton establishes his Adam and Eve firmly as characters, preserving a middle way between over-personalization, and over-allegorization.

In the events leading up to the Fall, Milton does portray Adam and Eve with some psychological naturalism. Personalities begin to develop. Various critics have taken these details as evidence of initial corruption on the part of Adam and Eve. Waldock writes:

> There is no way for Milton of making the transition from sinlessness to sin perfectly intelligible. It is obvious that Adam and Eve must already have contracted human weaknesses before they can start on the course of conduct that leads to their fall; to put it another way, they must already be fallen (technically) before they can begin to fall.[12]

In *Genesis*, as Tillyard observes,[13] the story is so brief that we accept that Eve is innocent until the precise moment of eating the apple. In a narrative poem, the incident is given much greater detail, is stretched over greater length, and the transition becomes a problem. Aware of this, Milton shows in Adam and Eve certain human emotional states that might lead to their fall; but that do not show them as fallen. The crux of Waldock's objection lies in the language of his argument; is it accurate to identify, as he does, 'human weaknesses' with being 'fallen'?

Man was created, God says, 'just and right, / Sufficient to have stood, though free to fall' (III.98-99). Raphael tells Adam, 'God made thee perfet, not immutable' (V.524). The mutability that man is given, the freedom, allows him to fluctuate from his initial perfection without actually or necessarily falling. Adam may love Eve too much, Eve may demand too much independence; these are departures from their 'perfection', evidence of their freedom, traits of independent personality—but they are not corruption. As H. V. S. Ogden points out in a valuable article,[14] these fluctuations from perfection can always be reversed—mutability, change, are allowed. Raphael can rebuke Adam for loving Eve too much, Adam can rebuke Eve for wanting to garden alone, and the rebukes could be acted upon. The Fall, though, the eating of the apple, is an irreversible act, and no matter how much repentance, no matter how much 'mutual accusation' (IX.1187), it cannot be changed.

12. A. J. A. Waldock, *Paradise Lost and Its Critics* (1947), p. 61.
13. E. M. W. Tillyard, *Studies in Milton* (1951), p. 10.
14. H. V. S. Ogden, 'The Crisis of *Paradise Lost* Reconsidered', *Philological Quarterly*, XXXVI (1957), 1-19.

Adam departs from his perfect state because of his passion for Eve. His equilibrium is disturbed so that the potentiality for disobedience to God is created. He becomes psychologically interesting, something more than a figure in a religious tableau or charade; he becomes more 'human'—and hence more vulnerable to weakness. The dangers of his passion are clear:

> when I approach
> Her loveliness, so absolute she seems
> And in her self complete, so well to know
> Her own, that what she wills to do or say
> Seems wisest, vertuousest, discreetest, best;
> All higher knowledge in her presence falls
> Degraded, Wisdom in discourse with her
> Loses discount'nanc't, and like folly shews;
> Autority and Reason on her wait,

(VIII.546-554)

Adam's love for Eve is beautifully evoked, but there is an excess in his passion. Milton suggests that by Adam's language, by the solecisms of 'vertuousest, discreetest', solecisms suggesting Adam's incoherence, his excessive praise, his groping for words; with wisdom discountenanced, words are hard to find. The excess of his passion is indicated when he testifies against himself by telling how 'higher knowledge . . . falls / Degraded' before her. The scheme of degree and hierarchy operated within man, as well as in the external universe. If the lower faculties of the body or the lower parts of the brain were taken notice of instead of the higher, then man would go astray. When reason becomes subservient to a lower faculty like passion, when authority waits on an inferior on whom it should be exercised, then the way is open for Adam to fall (as he says 'higher knowledge' does, without registering the implication for himself) 'Degraded'. 'Falls / Degraded' is proleptic of the fate of Adam and Eve, just as wisdom's becoming 'discount'nanc't' looks forward to Eve's return from having eaten the fruit. She returns 'with Countnance blithe' (IX.886), but Adam's moving response to seeing her is 'How art thou lost, how on a sudden lost, / Defac't, deflowrd, and now to Death devote' (IX.900-901). 'Guiltiness', Milton wrote in *De Doctrina Christiana* I.xii, 'accordingly, is accompanied or followed by terrors of conscience . . . whence results a diminution of the human countenance, and a conscious degradation of mind'.[15] The neo-Platonic idea of the face expressing the soul provides a basic image in the poem, for man as well as Satan.

The Fall is presaged—but certainly has not occurred. Adam can

---

15. Milton, *Works* (ed., F. A. Patterson) (Columbia edn, New York, 1933), XV.205. *See* Christopher Ricks, *Milton's Grand Style* (1963), p. 140.

still change. Raphael tells him in reply 'In loving thou dost well, in passion not' (VIII.588). But although Raphael may be expounding a great truth, a great commonplace, Adam is no more to be condemned or derided than he is to be held fallen. The dialogue has established the tragic tension of the situation—a tension that we find later when Adam has to decide whether or not to follow Eve in eating the fruit. It is the tension of acting in accord with the ordered, right way of going about things, and of the appeal of what is attractive yet said to be wrong. Neither way is easy—to follow the ordered way demands not a comfortable conservatism, but a rigorous discipline; to follow the wrong thing demands—as in Adam's decision to die with Eve—a courage. At this stage of the poem when Adam talks with Raphael, it is hard to say Adam's fully understandable passion for Eve is sinful. He may be failing to observe due order in things, but he is not corrupt. Milton makes him psychologically interesting, without making him fallen. It is not till he eats the fruit that he falls.

It is from this passion for Eve that Adam finally does fall, however. He chooses to follow her rather than his reason, rather than God's orders—the inferior rather than the superior. Milton has made Adam's motives in making the wrong choice quite clear. There was a choice to be made, and it was not an easy one.

Milton intended a tension between the appeal of an ordered harmonious universe, and the appeal of the individualistic, disruptive emotions. Satan is admirable for his courage, bravery, defiance of authority; Adam is admirable in his love for Eve. But to act as they did was to fall from the harmonious perfection. There is a tension between love and obedience, passion and reason, individualism and authority—and it is a tension that involves the reader. Milton is too honest to offer only the appeals of a traditional, ordered world; to have done that *would* have been to erect a monument to dead ideas.

As the weaker of the two, Eve has been more vulnerable to temptation from her creation. Her first action after her creation sensitively catches this. She lies down beside a lake and—

> As I bent down to look, just opposite,
> A Shape within the watry gleam appear'd
> Bending to look on me, I started back,
> It started back, but pleas'd I soon returnd,
> Pleas'd it returnd as soon . . .
>
> (IV.460-464)

Her delight with her own reflection reminds us of the myth of Narcissus. But Milton avoids an explicit comparison because, as

Harding points out[16] he does not want to suggest that Eve is sinfully vain; instead he is creating a suggestion of her potentiality for vanity—and the serpent is able to exploit that. She is not fallen, yet might easily. The whole incident is beautifully ambivalent, in that Eve's very naïvety (in not knowing the shape is her reflection) testifies to her innocence, yet the same naïvety causes her wonder and fascination with herself, suggesting her potential weakness.

The portrayal of Eve was one of Milton's greatest achievements. After the grandeur, bravery, nobility of Satan, after the evocation of Satan's great size, strength and suffering, Milton is able to offer the amazing contrast of the beautiful, slender, delicate, fragile Eve—so human in her behaviour, in her feelings, her arguments, her vulnerability: 'O much deceiv'd, much failing, hapless *Eve*' (IX.404). After the unique evocation of the great dimensions of the cosmic drama, the suggestion of infinite space, the huge panoramic visions, the 'gigantick loftiness' that Dr Johnson felt was Milton's 'natural port', comes the equally natural domestic drama of Book IX. The issues are general, for the discussion between Adam and Eve is one recurrent in every domestic situation: yet the issues are dramatized through fully realized individual characters. Eve suggests gardening apart from Adam in order to work more efficiently; but when Adam resists her suggestion, because of the danger from Satan, the discussion develops into one of principle. Eve—

> As one who loves, and som unkindness meets,
> With sweet austere composure thus repli'd.
>
> (IX.271-272)

Milton catches brilliantly the way she is surprised, even hurt, at Adam's reaction, the way she prickles at the imagined rebuke: she puts a sort of reproach into her voice yet replies as if nothing has happened, her composure so sweet and austere as to insist that something *has* happened, to warn Adam not to try it on again. But he does. And the issue of gardening becomes in itself unimportant, merely the chance event from which to develop their arguments of principle. It becomes a conflict of individuals for their own integrity, preserving their positions and independence within their marriage. Adam is sure there is danger in gardening alone, and he must persuade Eve that as the stronger and wiser he knows best: Eve 'thought / Less attributed to her Faith sincere' (IX.319-320) and so needs to prove herself. They are not quarrelling. But in order to preserve the equilibrium of their union Adam needs to insist on his authority which is weakened by her demand for independence;

16. Davis P. Harding, *The Club of Hercules: studies in the classical background of Paradise Lost*, pp. 73-5.

Eve needs to establish her self-sufficiency, her importance as an individual on her own, which are restricted by Adam's authority. Milton understands the basic dynamics of matrimony just as deeply as he understands in Satan the dynamics of rebellion. And of out the simple, domestic event, he shows how the Fall develops.

Eve's decision to garden alone obviously allows Satan a much better chance of success. As Adam is her superior, in intelligence and in the hierarchy, Eve should not insist on separation if he says it is unwise. And Adam can be blamed—indeed Eve later does so blame him— for letting her go instead of enforcing her stay; but his rule is to be with 'gentle sway', he cannot coerce. Looking back after the Fall, we can see what should or should not have happened; we can point to Eve's pride and desire for independence, to Adam's abnegation of authority; at the time, though, the situation seemed very different. To have put any sinister interpretation on the event as it occurred would have needed minds already fallen.

The break in the order and hierarchy caused by Eve's independence produces a break in their union. The 'hand in hand' image is fractured. As Eve leaves Adam, 'from her Husbands hand her hand / Soft she withdrew' (IX.385-386). It is a beautiful sentence, the lingering withdrawal in all its poignancy (it is the last time they will hold hands unfallen) is brought out by the catching repetition of 'hand her hand'—suggesting the slow drawing away.

The poignancy of the parting is enhanced by the beauty of Eve,

> like a Wood-Nymph light
> *Oread* or *Dryad*, or of *Delia*'s Train,
>
> (IX.386-387)

a beauty not so much described as implied by her comparison to classical figures, and by Adam's reaction:

> Her long with ardent look his Eye persu'd
> Delighted, but desiring more her stay.
> Oft he to her his charge of quick returne
> Repeated, shee to him as oft engag'd
> To be returned by Noon amid the Bowr,
>
> (IX.397-401)

He makes the parting linger on, calling out to her till she is out of sight or hearing, keeping in touch with her by voice and eye (though no more by hand) until she finally disappears.

Our next sight of Eve, a few lines later, is through Satan's eyes, when she stands, half-hidden amongst the roses, tending her flowers (IX.425). The flowers create not only Eve's beauty, by association, but also by their fragility and transience, heighten the poignancy of the scene. And even before we saw Eve in the garden, her tragedy was foretold, when Eden was contrasted with Enna:

> Not that faire field
> Of *Enna*, where *Proserpin* gathring flowrs
> Her self a fairer Flowre by gloomie *Dis*
> Was gatherd, . . .

(IV.268-271)

Eve like Proserpin is young and beautiful as a flower, each gathers flowers and by doing so augments her own beauty, each herself is gathered like a flower by a dark power coming from the underworld; as Empson pointed out in *Some Versions of Pastoral*, the allusions here are pointed and relevant, and they combine, with the poignancy of the Proserpin incident and the poignancy of having Eve's fall presaged in the first description of Paradise, to make the passage so memorable, one of the touchstones of great poetry for Matthew Arnold. The syntactical structure insists on the tragic irony: 'gathring flowrs / Her self a fairer Flowre / . . . was gatherd'. It is a pattern of great emotional force.

And it recurs just after Eve has left Adam to garden alone, in a subtle variation. Like Proserpin, Eve is tending flowers, and through her association with the flowers of the garden is seen as one—as the fairest—herself. So, 'oft stooping to support / Each Flowr' (IX.427-428):

> them she upstayes
> Gently with Mirtle band, mindless the while,
> Her self, though fairest unsupported Flowr,
> From her best prop so farr, and storm so nigh.

(IX.430-433)

The pattern earlier was a simple tragic irony—the gatherer gathered; like Marvell's Mower who, scything the grass, scythes down himself 'by careless chance'. It is rather like Satan's evil recoiling on himself—though qualified since Proserpin is a woman, delicate, beautiful, innocent. In this second passage, however, there is none of the possible implication of 'hoist with his own petard'. Instead, Eve is shown as being spontaneously kind, and the poignancy comes from the fact that there is no one there to be kind to her: 'Propping flowers / herself the fairest flower / herself *un*propped'. The wit of the earlier passage is modulated into tragedy by the negative prefix here—'fairest *un*supported Flowr' (my italics). The gatherer gathered has become the supporter *un*supported. All the implications of the Proserpin story that were introduced to us before we had even seen Eve, are now brought into play. They prefigured the tragedy and now, as we prepare for it, we remember the earlier reference: Proserpin's tragedy is echoed in Eve's—but by that subtle syntactic modification, Eve's is shown to be even more tragic, she is even more innocent, and even more outraged. Although in the scheme of degree, Eve is a lesser figure than Adam, Milton does not treat her fall as merely preparatory to Adam's. It is something far more than merely an event leading up to Adam's fall, it is an episode treated much more fully, much more richly, than his. Eve's fall is created as a tragedy in itself, and Eve is created as a fully human figure in the tragedy.

It takes the serpent some time to gain Eve's attention. She is used to the friendly animals of Paradise disporting around her, and paying reverence to her in accord with the natural hierarchy. Hence when the serpent 'bowd ... / Fawning, and lickd the ground whereon she trod' (IX.524-526) there was nothing unnatural in his action. Nor was there any reason for her to suspect him of evil: Raphael described the serpent at the creation as 'suttl'st Beast of all the field'(VII.495), yet at the same time went out of his way to emphasize that it was 'to thee / Not noxious, but obedient at thy call' (VII.497-498). His comment can only further have deceived Eve and encouraged her to trust the serpent. Earlier the narrator had remarked on the serpent's 'insinuating' movement, claiming he 'of his fatal guile / Gave proof unheeded' (IV.348-350). But why should an innocent Eve suspect evil in the innocence of Paradise? More of a problem is why the serpent should have been put into the garden: the 'fittest Imp of fraud' he is called (IX.89)—an odd inmate of Eden; and just as oddly the serpent is condemned afterwards (X.164) although it was only used by Satan. Of course, the Biblical myth is puzzling here—but Milton does not attempt to conceal the difficulties.

The serpent's appeal is by flattery; as the animals always fawn on man, this is hard to detect, though licking the ground is perhaps excessive. The shift from what is natural worship to flattery is brilliantly made. The serpent says that Eve is 'Fairest resemblance of thy Maker fair' (IX.538) which might mean that she is fairest and Adam is strongest; but it might also mean that she is fairest in everything, which in the order of things she is not, and should not want to be. From this ambiguity there is an easy transition to calling her 'A Goddess among Gods' (IX.547), then 'Empress of this fair World' (IX.568) which might just be true as she does 'rule' Paradise, and finally 'Queen of this Universe' (IX.684). This is not due reverence of beast for man, but elevating her to the status of a god.

That is what she wants. 'Be henceforth among the Gods / Thy self a Goddess', was the temptation in her dream. 'Ye shall be as Gods', the serpent tells her, following the *Genesis* temptation, 'Knowing both Good and Evil' (IX.709). We can argue that Eve should not want to become a god, that it is aspiring above her station. Yet Raphael says to Adam that they may become like gods—so making it a legitimate ambition: 'Your bodies may at last turn all to Spirit, / Improv'd by tract of time, and wingd ascend / Ethereal, as wee, or may at choice / Here or in Heav'nly Paradises dwell' (V.497-500). Empson, in his brilliant analysis of the Fall, makes much of the echo by Raphael of Satan's words in Eve's dream (V.79)—'the startling repetition of "as wee", again surrounded by commas and given Milton's double "E" for emphasis, only four hundred lines later. Eve is meant to prick up her ears at this, and so are we . . .'[17]

Even if we do not accept the significance of this verbal echo, or Empson's claim that God has arranged the correspondence and so 'made it baffling for her to gauge his intentions', Raphael's speech is certainly an encouragement to Adam and Eve to become like gods. If eating the fruit will produce that effect, perhaps they should eat it. How—and this is where the dream is really confusing— is Eve to distinguish between Raphael and the figure in the dream, 'One shap'd and wingd like one of those from Heav'n / By us oft seen; his dewie locks distilld / Ambrosia' (V.55-57)? Certainly the serpent is less resplendent—but perhaps God is tempting her courage; to become like a god one would need courage. If Raphael is sent to tell Adam and Eve that they will be like gods, why not believe someone who tells them *how* to be like gods?

The temptation of Eve is the last time we see the beauties of un-fallen Paradise, and the tragedy of the Fall is brought out by Milton's insistence on the ideal beauties of all the senses that are soon to be lost. The scene is vivid with colour. The serpent, 'Carbuncle his Eyes; / With burnisht Neck of verdant Gold', is not gaudy but beautiful, 'never since of Serpent kinde / Lovelier' (IX.500-505). Eve is discovered only half seen, 'so thick the Roses bushing round / About her glowd', and her beauty is augmented by her tending flowers of every colour, 'Carnation, Purple, Azure, or spect with Gold' (IX.426ff.). But as well as colour (and there are various greens offsetting the vivid flowers, 'Cedar, Pine or Palm'), the sense of smell is involved. Eve is 'Veild in a Cloud of Fragrance' (IX.425), suggesting that her innocence is protected by the scents of Paradise, and reminding us of the scents Satan notices on his first approach to the garden (IV.156ff.); in the ensuing simile comparing Satan to the town-dweller escaped into the country, Milton evokes 'The smell of Grain, or tedded Grass or Kine / Or Dairie' (IX.450-451).

The most vivid of these sensuous evocations, however, is given by the serpent as part of his seduction of Eve. It is a passage that makes

17. William Empson, *Some Versions of Pastoral* (1935), p. 150.

Leavis' claim that Milton's imagery is so inferior to Keats' ridiculous.[18] Satan addresses Eve in direct conversation, with a remarkable simplicity, contrasting strongly with the earlier artful and artificial rhetoric by which he seduced the angels (V.772ff.); the simplicity is its cunning.

> . . . on a day roving the field, I chanc'd
> A goodly Tree farr distant to behold
> Loaden with fruit of fairest colours mixt,
> Ruddie and Gold: I nearer drew to gaze;
> When from the boughes a savourie odour blown,
> Grateful to appetite, more pleas'd my sense
> Than smell of sweetest Fenel, or the Teats
> Of Ewe or Goat dropping with Milk at Ev'n,
> Unsuckt of Lamb or Kid, that tend thir play.
> To satisfie the sharp desire I had
> Of tasting those fair Apples, I resolv'd
> Not to deferr; hunger and thirst at once,
> Powerful persuaders, quickend at the scent
> Of that alluring fruit, urg'd me so keen.
> About the mossie Trunk I wound me soon,
>
> (IX.575-589)

The first description of the fruit is general—'fairest colours'—partly because the serpent is claiming to be seeing it from a distance, and partly to allow Eve to create her own picture of a beauty that will appeal to her from the serpent's hints, and partly to avoid making it obvious at this point that it is the forbidden fruit. To avoid that, the serpent never actually describes the fruit—they are fair, they are alluring. 'Alluring' may sound merely general, vague, imprecise— as he intends. But ironically it carries a subordinate and hidden meaning very precisely relevant to the situation: a lure was an apparatus used by falconers to attract their hawks back to them; and Satan has been trying to 'lure' Eve's eye already (IX.518); the fruit is a bait by which to trap her.

The first sight of it was of something 'Ruddie and Gold'. 'Gold' suggests the whole aureate, formalized description of the garden, the 'vegetable Gold' (IV.220) of the 'Tree of Life'. Satan does not develop that aspect, having once suggested it; he takes his key instead from 'Ruddie' with its more homely associations. And the fruit is then evoked not by any description—Satan cunningly avoids describing it—but by the tangential image of rural bliss. The implication is that the fruit shares the same innocence and peacefulness, will evoke the same response. So he creates the picture of the calm evening, the innocence of the 'Lamb or Kid' and their

18. F. R. Leavis, *The Common Pursuit* (1952), pp. 16-17.

innocent playing, the promise of milk for them from the full udders of their mothers, and later the peaceful 'mossie' tree. It is a picture of untroubled ease and innocence. Yet Satan is still as evasive as ever—he cannot be specific as to whether it is ewe or goat, lamb or kid he is describing.

The image is of richness, fullness, as well as of innocence and contentment. It is a vision of plenty—'the Teats / Of Ewe or Goat *dropping* with Milk at Ev'n'. And the suggestion is that the fruit must be eaten just as the teats must be sucked, to produce a relief for the ewe or goat as well as for the young lamb's or kid's thirst. The combination of this tactile suggestion, together with the smell (fennel, incidentally, is not merely a fragrant plant used in sauces, but traditionally a food of snakes), excite the idea of taste. The smoothness of the milk is a sensation that clashes with the acidity of the fruit—an acidity brought out by the suggestions in '*sharp* desire', 'keen' and 'quickend'. By the contrasting taste suggestions, Milton is able to tickle the salivary glands—just as sucking a lemon in front of a brass band proverbially stops the musicians from playing. Eliot's claim that Milton's verse shows a 'hypertrophy of the auditory imagination at the expense of the visual and tactile' surely cannot be sustained against passages like this.[19]

When Eve sees which tree it is that Satan is extolling, she resists his suggestions of eating the fruit. But already his flattery has begun to overpower her reason; when he first spoke 'Into the Heart of *Eve* his words made way, / Though at the voice much marveling.' (IX.550-551). Her reaction is two-fold—she receives his words, and marvels that he can speak. But her response, significantly, is not to the words that have entered her heart: being called 'A Goddess among Gods' (IX.547) echoes the tempter of her dream saying 'among the Gods / Thy self a Goddess' (V.77-78)—a remarkable echo. But she chooses to respond only to the more trivial fact that he can speak—a fact expressed in a subordinate clause in her reaction, not in a balanced doublet.

At the tree, the serpent's words find too ready an acceptance from her, they 'Into her heart too easie entrance won' (IX.734). He has brilliantly put up all the traditional objections to the myth of the forbidden tree—and indeed they are impressive. Why has God forbidden this one tree—'will God incense his ire / For such a petty Trespass' . . . 'God therefore cannot hurt ye, and be just; / Not just, not God' . . . 'to keep ye low and ignorant, / His worshippers' . . . 'can envie dwell / In heav'nly brests?' (IX.692 . . . 730). It is a marvellous tissue of argument, shifting ground continually between

19. T. S. Eliot, 'Milton I' in *On Poetry and Poets* (1957), p. 143.

postulates of a benevolent God who will not punish her, and a malevolent one who need not be obeyed.

As for the threat of Death, he dismisses that with the same sweep of rhetoric, giving her no time to reply to him or question his statements, giving no arguments but juggling instead with a quick thrust of rhetorical questions, playing with the key words 'Death'—'Die'—'Fruit'—'Life'—'Knowledge'. It is a brilliant piece of suasive rhetoric:

> do not believe
> Those rigid threats of Death; ye shall not Die:
> How should ye? by the Fruit? it gives you Life
> To Knowledge: By the Threatner? look on mee,
> Mee who have toucht and tasted, yet both live,
> And life more perfet have attaind than Fate
> Meant mee, by ventring higher than my Lot.
>
> (IX.684-690)

He gives no *reasons* why she will not die—Eve neglects to notice that, so carried away is she. She does not realize he is lying and never has eaten the fruit. The passage also contains a fine dramatic irony. 'Look on me:' she does not realize, though the reader does—that this is Satan, foremost of the angels once, reduced now to a serpent; that was what happened to him 'by ventring higher than my Lot', that is the 'life more perfet' resulting from his disobedience. The irony is enforced when God turns him into a serpent in Hell (X.514), and Satan involuntarily becomes what he lyingly claimed he was to Eve: the lie has recoiled on him.

Finally, Eve looks on the fruit 'which to behold / Might tempt alone'. For the first time it has become 'a provoking object', tempting not in itself, but because Eve has let the serpent's words win 'into her heart too easie entrance'.[20]

> Meanwhile the hour of Noon drew on, and wak'd
> An eager appetite, rais'd by the smell
> So savourie of that Fruit, which with desire,
> Inclinable now grown to touch or taste,
> Solicited her longing eye; . . .
>
> (IX.739-743)

To call this the sin of greed, as Tillyard does is surely ridiculous.[21] The whole poignancy of the Fall, the whole tragedy, is created by the naturalness of the events that aid it; it is so human a touch that Eve should be getting hungry at this point; it is time to eat.

20. *See* Dennis H. Burden, *The Logical Epic* (1967), p. 124ff.
21. E. M. W. Tillyard, *Milton* (1930), p. 260.

That is one of the trivialities of human life that tragically tips the balance.

Moreover we have seen eating not just as a basic drive, but as an image of the natural process of the whole universe—Raphael has been quite definite about that. Eating is natural, abstention from food at the due time (and it is the due lunch-time) would be unnatural. The cumulative emphases on the good of knowledge, the desirability of becoming God-like, the naturalness of eating, combine to encourage the disobedience; but not to make it inevitable. As D. H. Burden points out, 'her hunger is not ungovernable, nor does she have to eat of that particular Tree'.[22]

The serpent appeals to Eve by suggesting the knowledge that eating the fruit will give her; neither his nor her emphasis is on knowledge for itself, but on peripheral advantages. Eve seeks knowledge because she thinks it will make her like the gods. And the quest for knowledge is not even a distorted motive in Adam's fall. Afterwards he claims it was, saying to Michael he 'sought / Forbidden knowledge by forbidden means' (XII.278-279). But this was not something he considered before eating.

Milton's belief in the value of knowledge might easily have run counter to the myth of the forbidden tree of knowledge. His attack on censorship, his defence of freedom to read in *Areopagitica* (1644), is often quoted in this context:

I cannot praise a fugitive and cloistered virtue, unexercised and unbreathed, that never sallies out and sees her adversary, but slinks out of the race, where that immortal garland is to be run for, not without dust and heat. Assuredly we bring not innocence into the world, we bring impurity much rather; that which purifies us is trial, and trial is by what is contrary.[23]

But this defence of knowing evil in order to do right is a defence for fallen man—'assuredly we bring not innocence into the world'. Before the Fall, the state of Adam and Eve was very different, they *had* brought innocence with them. Satan suggests to Eve that evil can be better avoided if it is known (IX.698-699). It is Milton's own belief in *Areopagitica*, but a belief addressed to fallen man. Ironically, as Satan is fallen it is the sort of good advice he might well give; tragically, it is advice he gives to the innocent who have no need of knowing evil.

It is difficult to make this distinction clear to fallen readers; and Milton's method is to avoid emphasizing the magical knowledge-conferring powers of the tree. In so far as they remain, 'knowledge' is ambiguous: there is knowledge of everything—God's omniscience;

22. *The Logical Epic*, p. 124ff.
23. Burton, p. 158.

and there is the knowledge of evil, the experience of having sinned. By eating the fruit Adam and Eve gain the second knowledge, not the first. God has perhaps not been totally honest with Adam and Eve in using the word 'knowledge' equivocally—especially when Raphael encourages Adam in his pursuit of knowledge, within bounds.

The point that Milton emphasizes is that it is *forbidden* knowledge, and the emphasis is so heavily on the forbidden as to divert us from speculating about the knowledge. We are given, as Grierson remarked 'an arbitrary command, a tabu'.[24] And Milton himself testified to the arbitrariness:

It was necessary that something should be forbidden or commanded as a test of fidelity, and that an act in its own nature indifferent, in order that man's obedience might be thereby manifested. (*De Doctrina Christiana* I.x.[25])

Milton treated the myth not as about the acquisition of forbidden knowledge, but as about disobedience. The fruit of the tree seems to have given Adam and Eve little—they knew things before, they were learning; it is a 'fallacious Fruit' (IX.1046). But by the act of disobedience, by eating when forbidden, Adam and Eve sinned and so came to know good and evil, losing their innocence. It is in this simple disobedience, not in any Promethean quest for knowledge, that we must find the causes of the Fall.

Eve's fall itself is described not by great sonorities, not by the mighty rhetoric that was used to plan it in the first two books, but by a remarkable simplicity—emphasizing how slight, how trivial was the action of eating the fruit:

> So saying, her rash hand in evil hour
> Forth reaching to the Fruit, she pluckd, she eat:
> Earth felt the wound, and Nature from her seate
> Sighing through all her Works gave signs of woe,
> That all was lost. Back to the Thicket slunk
> The guiltie Serpent, and well might, for *Eve*
> Intent now wholly on her taste, naught else
> Regarded.

                                          (IX.780-787)

The action takes only two lines to relate; the consequences are immeasurable—and they are hinted at with a striking brevity in the simple, unamplified suggestion of how Earth and nature reacted. The supreme stroke is the reference to the serpent here, the description that he 'slunk' as if even he is horrified at what he has done,

24. H. J. C. Grierson, *Milton and Wordsworth: Poets and Prophets* (1937), p. 96.
25. *De Doctrina Christiana* I.Ch.X, *Works* (ed., F. A. Patterson) (Columbia edn, New York, 1933), XV, pp. 113-15.

as if aware that he is 'guiltie'. And the colloquial, casual 'and well might' brilliantly catches Eve's own casualness; she is unaware of the serpent, unaware of anything except eating.

Similarly when she returns to Adam attention is focused not on any great destruction of the world, not on any resonating grief, but on that garland he has woven for her, the garland no longer appropriate, the garland that when she comes, he drops. The cosmic tragedy is realized in these small and human details.

Eve approaches Adam with fallen dissimulation; theatrical metaphors applied earlier to Satan ('his Proem tun'd', IX.549; 667-8) are now descriptive of Eve. 'in her face Excuse / Came Prologue, and Apologie to prompt' (IX.854-855). Adam, however, avoids dissimulation; he says nothing, speaking first of all inwardly to himself; his decision is accomplished rapidly. 'Submitting to what seemd remediless' (and Lewis emphasizes that it only 'seemd'[26]) Adam says:

> with thee
> Certain my resolution is to Die;
> How can I live without thee, how forgoe
> Thy sweet Converse and Love so dearly joind,
> To live again in these wilde Woods forlorn?
>
> (IX.906-910)

At this stage the woods are not wild or forlorn: after the Fall they will be, and tragically Adam's decision to die with Eve is a decision that will make them so. But tragically, without Eve the woods would be wild and forlorn, no matter how paradisal, for him. Unable to live without her, he will die with her; the decision is hardly logical— nor is his toying with the unjustified comfort that God surely will not destroy them 'lest the Adversary / Triumph', (IX.947-948) toying with the idea that if the serpent has eaten of the fruit already, the crime may not be so bad.

These are not speculations that at all affect Adam's decision, anyway; as St Paul had said in I *Timothy* II:14, 'Adam was not deceived'. His reason was not overthrown. He knew his error: but decided to die so as not to live without Eve. Eve rejoices 'O glorious trial of exceeding Love' (IX.961). It *is* that of course; but the line, as Bush has pointed out, 'at once evokes the infinite contrast between Adam's misguided love and the love of Christ for man'.[27] It is a pregnant contrast: Adam's love is glorious, but it is a love that condemns all mankind, whereas Christ's redeems all mankind. It is certainly as Eve says a 'happie trial of thy Love' (IX.975)—but it had also been

26. *A Preface to Paradise Lost*, p. 123.
27. Douglas Bush, *Paradise Lost in Our Time* (1945), p. 107.

a trial of his obedience and virtue. It seems inappropriate to claim as baldly as does C. S. Lewis[28] that Adam fell by uxoriousness; there is no need to denigrate his love. It is excessive and inordinate, yet it is also what remains of the full love of their unfallen union. It is genuine love—but a love that has to exclude other considerations in order to persist, that has to exclude 'better knowledge'. Adam is aware of what has to be excluded:

> he scrupl'd not to eat
> Against his better knowledge, not deceiv'd,
> But fondly overcome with Femal charm.

> (IX.997-999)

He has to make a conscious decision of will to ignore his better knowledge. Waldock took exception to the last line, seeing in it Milton denigrating Adam's action.[29] Certainly Adam acted foolishly, 'fondly'; to ignore better knowledge and reason necessarily makes him act so. But fondly also means affectionately—and Adam's whole dilemma is expressed in the ambiguity.

It is not suggested that Eve persuaded him by argument at this moment. The 'charm' goes back to 'the charm of Beautys powerful glance' (VIII.533) that Adam told Raphael upset his reason; it has been a charm exercised over him ever since Eve's creation, a cumulative charm. Again an ambiguity indicates his dilemma; it is both a bewitching charm, a magic, an enchantment—something not good but at the same time difficult to escape from; and a strong attraction with no pejorative associations of magic or bewitching. Milton does not put the weight on one alternative rather than the other; he insists instead on the tension—the fond affection against foolish disobedience, succumbing to an irrational bewitching against responding to Eve's attractiveness. It is because of this tension that the Fall has its tragic power. Adam should not have let his reason be dominated by inferior faculties, ideally: ideally he should not follow Eve, who is his inferior. But the human force—and relevance— of the story arises because there was this tension.

The immediate results of Eve's fall are a sort of drunkenness— 'hightend as with Wine, jocond and boon' (IX.793). Her intemperance—'Greedily she ingorg'd without restraint' (IX.791)—is a sign of her fallen state both in her passions and appetites having taken control over her, and in her intoxication. Milton's emphasis on the drunkenness is important; it allows Eve to be blasphemous in referring to God as 'our great forbidder', stupid in imagining God may not have noticed, idolatrous in her worship of the tree, jealous

28. *A Preface to Paradise Lost*, p. 122.
29. *Paradise Lost and Its Critics*, pp. 48-50.

and what Lewis has called murderous[30] in her decision that Adam must die with her rather than have another Eve.

We do not, however, think of this as cold-blooded murder as we read, because of Eve's evident intoxication. All her actions and statements here are certainly sinful, but when the effect of the fruit wears off, the suggestion is, she will sober up and come to her senses. This is what happens; the drunkenness analogy allows her to be uninhibitedly fallen, immediately and suddenly corrupt in a naturalistically explained way; and also excessively yet not permanently corrupt. Similarly when Adam has eaten 'As with new Wine intoxicated both / They swim in mirth' (IX.1008-1009); again the drunkenness is naturalistically portrayed. Adam becomes the life of the party: 'if such pleasure be / In things to us forbidden, it might be wisht / For this one Tree had bin forbidden ten' (IX.1024-1026). His wit here—and it is funny—is so hideously out of place, he is so mindlessly unaware of what he is doing, that the whole tragedy is underlined for us: the triviality of action that causes the ruin of mankind and the immediate trivialization of mind that Adam shows now he is fallen are painfully caught; we want to laugh at Adam's joke, but unlike Adam we can see the full consequences of his action.

It is hardly necessary to claim the fruit is an aphrodisiac as Peter does;[31] simply Adam and Eve rush off for drunken sex. 'now let us play', says Adam; he 'forbore not glance or toy' (IX.1027, 1034). The emphasis is on triviality. As Lewis says, 'Eve is becoming to him a *thing*'.[32] The sight of her beauties 'so enflame my sense / With ardor to enjoy thee' (IX.1031-1032)—his senses, not his love, are inflamed, and Eve is an object to be enjoyed, not an individual to love; Satan's flames are not an irrelevant association.

They awake with a hangover, perpetuating the drunkenness analogy. Everything seems different after the previous exhilaration. They,

> Soon found thir Eyes how opend, and thir minds
> How darkend; innocence, that as a veil
> Had shaddowd them from knowing ill, was gon,

> (IX.1053-1055)

Oddly, innocence as a veil suggests a merely temporary covering; it was inevitable that innocence, being only a veil, should be swept away. There is a parallel in the way Adam refers to covering 'Those

---

30. *A Preface to Paradise Lost*, pp. 121-2.
31. John Peter, *A Critique of Paradise Lost* (1960), p. 134.
32. *A Preface to Paradise Lost*, p. 124.

middle parts, that this new comer, Shame, / There sit not' (IX.1097-1098), as if shame, too, is external and superficial. Of course it is—and after Christ's redemption of man, after that final judgement, presumably it will be swept away. But the analogy of innocence as a veil suggests that it, too, was to be removed. It is one of those puzzling suggestions of the inevitability of the Fall, almost, indeed, of its necessity.

Fallen, Adam and Eve have lost the peace and happiness of their unity. They quarrel, 'in mutual accusation spent / The fruitless hours, but neither self-condemning' (IX.1187-1188). Fruitless contains a wealth of tragic, bitter irony. They feel alienated and estranged from each other, and estranged too, from God and the universe. The animals are no longer 'much in awe / Of Man, but fled him, or with count'nance grim / Glar'd on him passing' (X.712-714). Adam and Eve hide when God walks in the garden (X.100).

Adam's first speech after waking from the fallen sleep, begins 'O *Eve*, in evil hour thou didst give ear' (IX.1067) and for the first time, and now from henceforth unavoidably, the pun associates Eve's name with evil; it is the most cruel reproach. After his loving decision to die with her, to make that identification, and later to call her 'serpent' (X.867), come as a shock. His cruelty marks him as clearly fallen; the truth of the accusation marks her as fallen equally.

Before they were fallen, Adam and Eve were described naturally in ennobling terms. Adam smiles on Eve, for instance 'as *Jupiter* / On *Juno* smiles, when he impregns the Clouds / That shed *May* Flowers' (IV.499-501). After the Fall, however, they are both degraded, and are fittingly described in reducing images. Adam leaves Eve after that first fallen sleep, and—

> So rose the *Danite* strong
> *Herculean Samson* from the Harlot-lap
> Of *Philistean Dalilah*, and wak'd
> Shorn of his strength, . . .
>
> (IX.1059-1062)

The contrast with the manner in which they used to be described is huge.

Yet it is not a wholly belittling comparison. Samson is here shown degraded—yet he will regain a tragic nobility. So will Adam. On the other hand again, the image does remind us of that earlier implicit comparison of Satan to Samson (I.596). The associations are complex, ambivalent. The pattern of amplification-meiosis, hitherto necessarily limited to the fallen Satan, is now brought into play on man. Adam and Eve are like the savages discovered by Columbus after their Fall (IX.1116): it is a tragic contrast with their primitive innocence: yet the mention of Columbus may suggest fallen man's potential for courage and endeavour. And that, of course, reminds us of Satan's courageous voyage to discover Earth.

Not only is the pattern of amplification-meiosis now applied to man; man is now compared to Satan—in itself an example of the reductive comparison, but at the same time bringing into play as relevant to man all the ambiguities already applied to Satan. The narrator comments on the devils in Hell 'O how unlike the place from whence they fell!' (I.75)—and the phrase is echoed in form and meaning, implicitly comparing the fallen Adam and Eve to the fallen angels, when the narrator comments on them 'O how unlike / To that first naked Glorie' (IX.1114-1115). Adam's 'Abyss of fears' (X.842) is like Satan's 'in the lowest deep a lower deep / Still threatning to devour me' (IV.76-77).[33] When Adam has given his soliloquy, 'in a troubl'd Sea of passion tost', 'On the Ground / Outstretcht he lay, on the cold ground, and oft / Curs'd his Creation' (X.718, 850-852); it reminds us of Satan in Hell, 'stretcht out huge in length the Arch-Fiend lay / Chaind on the burning Lake' (I.209-210). Adam's 'troubl'd Sea' is an 'inward' one, Satan's is the burning lake, though he burns inside as much; Adam's ground is cold, Satan's burning—but Hell has hot and cold. It is hard to say who is suffering the least. The difference between them is that Satan is doomed, for Adam there is to be a redemption.

After the Fall Adam and Eve can be treated in the complex images that have been applied to Satan; but this is not merely a matter of imagery; because they are fallen, their natures are more complex. They now have a human richness of personality, a wider range of emotions and behaviour—abuse, grief, despair, fear. Arguments develop between them and issues arise—for instance, whether they should seek death so that they will have no offspring to suffer it too.

Their emotions and expressions of them now range from the extreme abyss of despair that Adam shows to the nobility of Eve's love. Adam cries out 'why do I overlive, / Why am I mockt with death, and lengthend out / To deathless pain?' (X.773-775). The imaginative coinage of 'overlive' and the enhancing suggestion of the image of Procrustes' bed give the grief a memorable expression. But man is capable of nobility, and Eve shows the way love will rescue them from the abyss, and offers, too, that the punishment should be hers alone:

> both have sinnd, but thou
> Against God onely, I against God and thee,
> And to the place of judgement will return,

33. *See* Isabel MacCaffrey, *Paradise Lost as 'Myth'* (1959), pp. 78, 117.

> There with my cries importune Heaven, that all
> The sentence from thy head remov'd may light
> On me, sole cause to thee of all this woe,
> Mee mee onely just object of his ire.
>
> (X.930-936)

Her language echoes Christ's at his sacrifice. Eve's love now is something very far removed from her decision to get Adam to die with her lest he should find another Eve.

Their reconciliation is a most moving scene. Eve's speech 'Forsake me not thus, *Adam*,' (X.914) has expressed beautifully her love for him and her terror of being separated from him—'Whither shall I betake me, where subsist?' (X.922). Eve's vulnerability and dependence are wonderfully created though they are usually less remarked on than Adam's bitter indictment of women and the suffering they bring to men (X.898-906). This passage has often been read as autobiographical: but just as strong as the hatred for women it expresses, is the ensuing love that Adam shows for Eve after her speech. If Milton's personality is to be found in the misogyny, it must also be recognized in the sensitive evocation of reconciliation and love that Adam's bitterness gives way to:

> soon his heart relented
> Towards her, his life so late and sole delight,
> Now at his feet submissive in distress,
> Creature so faire his reconcilement seeking,
> His counsel whom she had displeas'd, his aid;
> As one disarmd, his anger all he lost,
>
> (X.940-945)

Adam's deep love for and closeness to Eve is finely caught in such simple yet such imaginative phrases as 'his life so late and sole delight,' for she has been his life, and it was for life with her that he chose death; she was his sole delight—before her creation he was lonely—and he ate the fruit to avoid being left alive without her; and her physical attractiveness is simply caught in 'creature *so faire* his reconcilement seeking', the non-committal 'creature' softened and transformed by the adjective quietly placed after it. Milton has created, in the quarrel and the reconciliation, the complexity and richness of a human relationship.

What finally emerges at the end of Book X is a human dignity. Here Adam and Eve return to God instead of sinking deeper into the pit of despair and corruption like Satan. Adam rejects the idea of suicide; and he and Eve accept God's judgement, and by prayer hope to mollify it. The book ends with them both praying, and Book XI opens with the Son receiving the prayers, and presenting them

107

to God. 'See Father, what first fruits on Earth are sprung / From thy implanted Grace in Man' (XI.22-23). 'The fruitless hours' that closed Book IX in arguments have now borne fruit; indeed, eating the forbidden fruit has produced eventually a good fruit.

Milton's subject in *Paradise Lost* was announced in the opening lines:

> Of Mans First Disobedience, and the Fruit
> Of that Forbidden Tree, whose mortal taste
> Brought Death into the World, and all our woe,
> With loss of *Eden*, till one greater Man
> Restore us, and regain the blissful Seat,
> Sing Heav'nly Muse, . . .
>
> (I.1-6)

We have now seen the fruit of eating 'the Fruit of that Forbidden Tree'. They know evil, experience shame, guilt; their unity is gone, they quarrel; 'high Passions, Anger, Hate, / Mistrust, Suspicion, Discord, . . . shook sore / Thir inward State of Mind' (IX.1123-1125); they have to toil, to feel pangs of childbirth; they are to die; and Paradise is lost to them.

Yet we have seen good fruits resulting. And even in the opening lines the redemption that will follow is stated. In Book X God sees the evil that results from the Fall, sees Sin and Death advancing on Earth; he promises their destruction, 'and the heav'nly Audience loud / Sung *Halleluiah*' (X.641-642). But even as they are singing praise of God's goodness and justness, God is disordering the universe from its primal peacefulness, introducing seasons 'with cold and heat / Scarce tollerable' (X.653-654) to Earth, causing fierce winds to rise.

The Fall seems disastrous, but the angels' praise demonstrates how it leads in fact to greater goodness—to the final destruction of Sin and Death, and finally, to the redemption of man. We have, finally, the paradox of the *felix culpa*, the 'fortunate Fall': the conclusion that the Fall is in fact a happy event, because of the greater good of Christ's redemption of man and destruction of Sin and Death —events that would not have occurred had man not fallen. The most impressive expression of this is in Adam's speech, after Michael has told him of the crucifixion, resurrection and last judgement.

> O goodness infinite, goodness immense!
> That all this good of evil shall produce,
> And evil turn to good; more wonderful
> Than that which by creation first brought forth
> Light out of darkness! full of doubt I stand,

> Whether I should repent me now of sin
> By mee done and occasiond, or rejoice
> Much more, that much more good thereof shall spring,
>
> (XII.469-476)

Certainly Adam's outburst is joyous; certainly the poem has demonstrated this scheme of good from evil—creation has resulted from the revolt; and we are told of the redemption to result from the Fall. And yet the redemption is hardly created in the poem. As Kermode has suggested,[34] the loss of Paradise was a theme established and created through the senses; the assurance of redemption is an intellectual paradox dependent upon revelation. Milton does not create it, or even dramatize—he merely asserts that it will happen; whereas we have seen the sensual vividness of the lost garden. Indeed, Broadbent comments on Adam's words that, 'The lyric impulse is geared down into mechanics—"That all this good of evil shall produce, And evil turn to good"—as though the cosmos were a factory.'[35] Milton does not describe the crucifixion with any richness of emotion. Michael's few words about it seem to be covering the ground as briefly as possible, without passion, without evocation, almost perfunctorily:

> to death condemnd,
> A shameful and accurst, naild to the Cross
> By his own Nation, slaine for bringing Life;
> But to the Cross he nailes thy Enemies,
> The Law that is against thee, and the sins
> Of all mankind, with him there crucifi'd,
> Never to hurt them more who rightly trust
> In this his satisfaction; so he dies,
> But soon revives, Death over him no power
> Shall long usurp; . . .
>
> (XII.412-421)

The scheme of redemption is *stated*; but the crucifixion and the harrowing of Hell, something that had been so great an inspiration to medieval literature, fail to move Milton to dramatize the scheme.

Certainly Eve's last word in the poem is 'restore'—'By mee the Promis'd Seed shall all restore' (XII.623), certainly Michael talks of the time when 'the Earth / Shall all be Paradise, far happier place / Than this of *Eden*' (XII.463-465). But there is a difference between the overall theological pattern of the idea of redemption, that Milton is including in his poem, and the poetic emphasis on the loss of Paradise. It is hard to see the poem as Marjorie Nicolson does—

34. Frank Kermode (ed.), *The Living Milton*, p. 121.
35. J. B. Broadbent, *Some Graver Subject* (1960), p. 283.

'not a tragedy but a divine comedy'.[36] Such a reading would have theological difficulties. As D. H. Burden remarks, 'Milton is worried about the idea of the "fortunate Fall". It is one thing to say that Adam is, as a result of the atonement, better off than he was in Paradise, but something altogether different to suggest that he is better off than he would have been if he had stayed obedient. God's mercy cannot be allowed to make nonsense of his justice.'[37] The vision of the postlapsarian world in the last two books is, after all, one that insists on the evil, on the loss of peace and innocence, on the destruction that result from the Fall. The poem's very title insists on the *loss* of Paradise.

But the tragedy and loss are not the total impression of the poem. We have seen Adam and Eve's return to God in prayer. The conclusion shows Adam and Eve descending from Paradise down the cliff, their descent metaphorical of their Fall, weeping—yet ready and able to endure the new world. The 'better fortitude / Of Patience and Heroic Martyrdom' (IX.31-32) is applicable not only to Christ, but to the new heroes Adam and Eve. It is a patience achieved after their despair in Book X, a patience advocated to Adam by Michael after the visions of death—visions that made Adam want to die quickly to avoid the pain of suffering. But Michael instructs him 'Nor love thy Life, nor hate; but what thou liv'st / Live well, how long or short permit to Heav'n' (XI.553-554). It is with this patience to the will of God that the poem ends, rather than any eager hope of restoration and redemption. There is a hope in the concluding lines of a fresh start, the world *is* all before them, they can begin again, certainly in worse conditions, but at least they can begin again. It is a hope—but not an expression of joy; the only expression of joy is of the joy that has passed, to the simplicity and innocence of 'thir happie seat' of Paradise. Although God will be with them on Earth, although the Fall will eventually produce good, the poem does not end with any great declaration of happiness.

> They looking back, all th' Eastern side beheld
> Of Paradise, so late thir happie seat,
> Wav'd over by that flaming Brand, the Gate
> With dreadful Faces throngd and fierie Arms:
> Som natural tears they dropd, but wip'd them soon;
> The World was all before them, where to choose
> Thir place of rest, and Providence thir guide:
> They hand in hand with wandring steps and slow,
> Through *Eden* took thir solitarie way.
>
> (XII.641-649)

36. Marjorie Nicolson, *Milton—a reader's guide* (1964), p. 322.
37. *The Logical Epic*, p. 37.

It is an ending of exquisite tact. In keeping with their fallen ambivalence, they are being driven out by 'The brandisht sword of God' (XII.633), yet protected by 'Providence thir guide'. The sadness of lost happiness, of the tears, the horror of the dreadful faces, is qualified because of the hope of the world before them. The solitariness—alienated from nature, disobedient to God, as yet without children, is qualified by the renewed image of their union 'hand in hand'; and, though alone, Providence is guiding them. The fact that they now have to toil and so will need 'rest' is augmented by the suggestion that the Earth will at least offer them a 'place of rest'—it is not thoroughly alien. The tragic notes are qualified into the ambivalent haunting chord of the simultaneous tragic loss and trusting hope. They are fallen, but not abandoned; Paradise is lost, but they are not.

CHAPTER V

The Critics

Addison expressed the eighteenth-century admiration for *Paradise Lost* in his *Spectator* essays of 1712. Milton's distinction, he wrote in *The Spectator*, No. 279, was that:

in the greatness of his sentiments he triumphs over all the poets both modern and ancient, Homer only excepted. It is impossible for the imagination of man to distend itself with greater ideas. . . .[1]

The epic greatness of his theme had, Dr Johnson pointed out, the additional advantage that 'the substance of the narrative is truth'. Some qualifications were made to the enthusiasm for the poem— Addison found Book VII 'wonderfully sublime' but lacking in action, and Johnson noted how the subject 'admits no human manners till the Fall' so that 'the want of human interest is always felt. *Paradise Lost* is one of the books which the reader admires and lays down, and forgets to take up again'.[2] But the advantage of the Biblical truth of the subject ensured the poem's high valuation.

But by the end of the eighteenth century, as beliefs in freedom and liberalism developed, as the security of an ordered, set society was challenged and the questioning of Christianity increased, a shift in attitude to *Paradise Lost* occurred. It was still held to be a great poem, not for the moral instruction, the obedience to God it recommended, or for its presentation of an hierarchical world-picture. First Blake and then Shelley gave voice to what became the Satanist reading of the poem. Interest centred on the defiant rebel—'my favourite hero' said Burns in 1787. In his *Lectures on the English Poets* (1818) Hazlitt wrote that he was 'ready to give up the dialogues in Heaven' and the war:

the interest of the poem arises from the daring ambition and fierce passions

1. Joseph Addison, *The Spectator*, No. 279.
2. Johnson, 'Milton' in *Lives of the English Poets* (World's Classics, 1952), I.120, 122, 127.

of Satan, and from the account of the paradisaical happiness, and the loss of it by our first parents.[3]

The Satanist reading was only possible because the 'theological understructure' of the poem had now crumbled. Since Blake, it has been a persistently offered account. The Victorian critic Walter Bagehot found a disjunction between the poem's 'theme' of obedience and Milton's 'real sympathy' making him 'side with the rebellious element'.[4] In the twentieth century critics such as Tillyard have developed this idea of a tension between Milton's expressed beliefs and the poem's 'unconscious meanings': in this latter group Tillyard includes Milton's sympathy for Satan, hostility towards woman, pessimism, lack of conviction in the delights of Paradise, and having 'no profound belief in the incarnate Christ'.[5]

E. M. W. Tillyard has argued that Milton's so called Arianism[6] was an unconscious meaning in *Paradise Lost*. C. S. Lewis, one of the twentieth century's main defenders of the poem's theological conventionality, has denied its presence. The unorthodoxy of Milton's beliefs was not known until 1825 when his *De Doctrina Christiana* was discovered and published. But significantly, its publication had little effect on Milton criticism of the time. The collapse of the theological understructure of *Paradise Lost* had led to Satanist sympathies unthinkable to Dr Johnson—but had led also to a lack of interest in the 'ideas' of the poem. Milton's 'philosophy, human and divine, may be tolerably understood by one not much advanced in years', Keats wrote in a letter to Reynolds in May 1818. *De Doctrina Christiana* provoked no stir of thought about Milton's ideas. A dissociation between the poetic technique and the themes had set in. The Victorian emphasis on the enchanting stylist arose: 'the underlying thoughts are few, though the flowers on the surface are so many', Bagehot wrote.[7] For Raleigh at the beginning of the twentieth century, *Paradise Lost* was 'a monument to dead ideas'.[8]

But with the revolutions in literary taste, its music became less

3. William Hazlitt, 'On Shakespeare and Milton' in *Lectures on the English Poets* (Everyman's Library, 1910), p. 63.
4. Walter Bagehot, 'Wordsworth, Tennyson and Browning . . .' (1864) in *Literary Studies* (Everyman's Library, 1911), Vol. II, p. 321.
5. E. M. W. Tillyard, *Milton* (1930), pp. 276, 279.
6. Arius, the presbyter of Alexandria in the 4th century AD denied that Christ was of one and the same substance or essence with God. W. R. Parker, *Milton* (1968), II.1057-8, denies that Milton was an Arian in any strict sense of the term, though 'unorthodox he certainly was'. Milton presents Christ as different from and inferior to the Father, but still of the divine substance.
7. 'Milton' in *Literary Studies* (Everyman's Library, 1911), I, p. 183.
8. Walter Raleigh, *Milton* (1900), p. 80.

enchanting. And then there was nothing left. The verse had always attracted some hostility. Addison had objected to the use of 'old words, transpositions and foreign idioms' and neither he nor Johnson liked Milton's word-play or Latinizations. Keats wrote in a letter of September 1819 that the poem was 'a curruption of our Language' but also 'a beautiful and grand Curiosity'. The attacks on Milton in the 1920s and 1930s, however, saw only the corruption and missed the beauty, and were extended much further than arguments about Latinity.

Two of the most important anti-Miltonists were the poets, Ezra Pound and T. S. Eliot, and their objections need to be seen not as overdue revelations of truth, but as part of the literary revolution they were engaged in. 'Milton is the worst sort of poison',[9] Pound wrote—but he was a 'poison' for young poets. The qualities Milton had were not those Pound and Eliot wanted to follow in their own verse. Milton's sonorous verse paragraphs, his organ voice, his generality, his remoteness from colloquial speech, his artificiality— all these qualities for which he had been valued he was now condemned. 'This', Dr Leavis wrote of a passage of Donne against which he compared Milton unfavourably, 'is the Shakespearian use of English; one might say that it is the English use—the use, in the essential spirit of the language, of its characteristic resources.'[10] Donne and the other Metaphysicals and Shakespeare were the models for and favourites of the early twentieth century.

It is easy to see what developed from this preference in taste. Milton was not like Donne or Shakespeare, so he was held to be unlike them in all the qualities that made them good—in all the essential qualities of English poetry—so the argument slid: Milton is general, incapable of concrete realization, lacks visual imagination, uses words for the sound not the meaning, his language is vague and imprecise, his syntax distant from speech and so cut off from the resources of the English language, his similes are vague, digressive, irrelevant, his verse lacks metaphorical life. A second line of attack was his unfortunate influence on later poets.

The case against Milton combined some accurate description elevated to value judgement, with some inaccurate assertion. In return the Miltonists offered little. 'Dr Leavis does not differ from me about the properties of Milton's epic verse. He describes them very accurately . . .' C. S. Lewis wrote. 'It is not that he and I see different things when we look at *Paradise Lost*. He sees and hates

9. *Literary Essays of Ezra Pound* (ed.) T. S. Eliot (1954), p. 216.
10. F. R. Leavis, *Revaluation* (1936), p. 55. The essay first appeared in *Scrutiny* in 1933.

the very same that I see and love.'[11] Lewis' *A Preface to Paradise Lost* (1942) is, despite its limitations, a very valuable study. Milton is writing an epic, he insists; to complain of the ritualistic style, and pomposity, is to complain of the essential nature of the secondary epic. Primary epic was delivered orally, accompanied by a musical instrument, in full ceremony. The style of secondary epic,

the Virgilian and Miltonic style is there to compensate for—to counteract— the privacy and informality of silent reading in a man's own study . . . To blame it for being ritualistic or incantatory, for lacking intimacy or the speaking voice, is to blame it for being just what it intends to be and ought to be.[12]

But this is an argument that does not fully engage with Leavis. Lewis offers the positive qualities of formality, ritual, and incantation. But cannot verse be at the same time ritualistic and sensitive, incantatory and linguistically daring, rich in complex imagery as well as noble in the sound of its paragraphs?

Gradually the presence of those qualities which Leavis had claimed Milton lacked, and which Lewis, Rajan and Muir had thought improper to look for, have been demonstrated in the verse of *Paradise Lost*. William Empson's essay in *Some Versions of Pastoral* had as early as 1935 shown how responsive *Paradise Lost* was to the close reading favoured by twentieth-century critics, and the poem was approached again from a similar standpoint by Cleanth Brooks in an article 'Milton and the New Criticism'.[13] Then the book-length studies of Broadbent, Stein, MacCaffrey, and Cope further demonstrated the sensitivity, richness and complexity of the verse. Finally in 1963 Christopher Ricks' *Milton's Grand Style* appeared, an account solely of the style, which, drawing on eighteenth-century as well as modern commentators, brilliantly demonstrated the subtleties and complexities of Milton's verse.

One of the basic objections to *Paradise Lost* was that Milton had achieved the general effects of the poem at the expense of detail, both of language and image. Eliot quoted the description of Satan on the burning lake in which he is compared to Leviathan:

> With Head up-lift above the wave, and Eyes
> That sparkling blaz'd, his other Parts besides
> Prone on the Flood, . . .
>
> (I.193-195)

and commented in his British Academy lecture on Milton:

11. C. S. Lewis, *A Preface to Paradise Lost* (1942), p. 130.
12. *A Preface to Paradise Lost*, p. 39.
13. Cleanth Brooks, 'Milton and the New Criticism', *Sewanee Review*, Winter 1951.

I am not too happy about eyes that both blaze and sparkle, unless Milton meant us to imagine a roaring fire ejecting sparks: and that is *too* fiery an image for even supernatural eyes. The fact that the lake was burning somewhat diminishes the effect of the fiery eyes; and it is difficult to imagine a burning lake in a scene where there was only darkness visible. But with this kind of inconsistency we are familiar in Milton.[14]

'These criticisms seem to me unanswerable', Leavis declared[15]— but they are criticisms based on a misreading. The 'darkness visible' (I.63) does not make it difficult to imagine a burning lake; the phrase is one of the recurrent oxymorons describing the unimaginable Hell, one whose ambiguities evoke the unknown world; the darkness is 'visible' in the sense that we can see it, a sort of tangible darkness like 'the palpable obscure' (II.406) or the 'light thickens' of Shakespeare's oncoming night. But it is also darkness we can see through—visible meaning in this sense not 'able to be seen' but also 'able to allow sight'. It is a darkness that darkens but does not black out—as is made quite clear in the phrase's full context—'yet from those flames / No light, but rather darkness visible / Serv'd onely to discover sights of woe' (I.62-64). Dr Johnson indicated that 'quality peculiar to infernal lustre, that its light fell only upon faults'.[16]

There is no confusion in seeing the burning lake through the darkness visible. And since the whole dungeon burns with these flames of darkness visible rather than with light, the fiery eyes stand out in distinct contrast, bright against that darkness. Nor is there any confusion in the 'Eyes / That sparkling blaz'd'. We have an imaginative condensation, not a failed equation as Eliot seems to read it. What would be sparkling in human eyes, in Satan blazed; eyes conventionally sparkle to show aliveness and liveliness—but Satan's energy is such that his eyes blaze; sparkling eyes express emotion, and Satan is in such great torment and full of such rage that the sparkles are in him flames. And Satan is physically huge, as the passage goes on to demonstrate with the Leviathan comparison, so that what would be sparkles in human eyes, proportionally for Satan's eyes blazed. It is a way of insisting here on Satan's greatness and of course on his glory. His eyes are so alive even when the rest of his body is chained 'Prone on the Flood'. The charges of imprecision cannot be sustained.

Satan's size is established by a comparison with

14. T. S. Eliot cut this passage from his lecture when it was reprinted as 'Milton II' in *On Poetry and Poets* (1957). The full text is reprinted in James Thorpe, *Milton Criticism* (1951).
15. F. R. Leavis, *The Common Pursuit* (1952), p. 15.
16. Samuel Johnson, *The Rambler*, No. 3.

> *Leviathan*, which God of all his works
> Created hugest that swim th' Ocean stream:
> Him haply slumbring on the *Norway* foam
> The Pilot of som small night-founderd Skiff,
> Deeming som Iland, oft, as Sea-men tell,
> With fixed Anchor in his scaly rinde
> Moors by his side under the Lee, while Night
> Invests the Sea, and wished Morn delays:
>
> (I.201-208)

Again Eliot finds objections of detail. He complains that in 'som small night-founderd Skiff'—'the literal meaning of *founder* immediately presents itself. A *foundered* skiff could not be *moored*, to a whale or to anything else.'[17] Leavis sees in this Milton's 'relaxed concern for meaning—for "the idea" . . . the weakness is profoundly characteristic, and it would be easy to find other instances demanding similar comment'.[18] That Leavis, instead of finding other instances, merely repeated those noted by Eliot, suggests such instances are not easy to find.

The sense of 'founder' meaning to sink was a seventeeth-century particularization of the wider meaning 'to plunge to the bottom'. It might be argued, against the charge of confusion, that this sense of 'sink' did not immediately present itself to a seventeenth-century reader since it was a recent particularization, and Milton has deliberately excluded it by forming the compound 'night-founderd'. 'Founder' has a well-established metaphorical meaning— 'our hopes are foundered'—and it is the metaphorical sense that is immediately present here. The ship has been sunk by night— it has been metaphorically 'plunged to the bottom'. It is not sunk by the sea pouring in, but figuratively by the night coming down. Eliot seems to have read the phrase as sunk *during* the night, rather than as sunk (figuratively) *by* the night. It is a small skiff, and the pilot is 'sunk' until morn comes and he can find out where he is. But when morn does come, the implication is, he will indeed be sunk, be literally plunged to the bottom. When the whale swims down beneath the surface, it will drag the ship after it. The literal meaning of 'founder' is present as an ironic prolepsis.

Eliot remarked, too, not only on the details of language but on the relevance of the simile, on

the happy introduction of so much extraneous matter. Any writer, straining for images of hugeness, might have thought of the whale, but only Milton could have included the anecdote of the deluded seamen without our wanting to put a blue pencil through it. We *nearly* forget Satan in attending

17. Thorpe, *Milton Criticism*, p. 327n.
18. *The Common Pursuit*, pp. 21-2.

to the story of the whale; Milton recalls us just in time. Therefore the diversion strengthens, instead of weakening, the passage.[19]

Eliot's manner is here evasive and his praise oddly damaging, as Leavis indicated:

To say that the diversion *strengthens* anything is inapt and misleading; Miltonic similes don't focus one's perception of the relevant, or sharpen definition in that way . . . We are happy about the introduction of so much extraneous matter, because the 'Miltonic music' weakens our sense of relevance, just as it relaxes our grasp of sense.[20]

The traditional defence of such similes was that they were 'Homeric' —befitting an epic poem, digressive. They had a point of comparison initially but were expanded, as for instance Lewis claimed of the comparison of the devils to elves, 'to provide contrast and relief, to refresh us by a transition from Hell to a moonlit English lane'.[21] B. A. Wright accounts for the Leviathan passage by saying that Milton wanted 'to create a vision of immensity and terror',[22] and so had to describe the immense object in detail in order to present a vivid picture to our imagination. It is a defence that plays into the anti-Miltonist hands: any vision of immensity would do—why are the details of the ship and 'wished Morn' there? Charming and decorative, such similes are hardly integral to the poem.

Christopher Ricks, however, pointed out that the Leviathan simile is not simply vague and digressive. 'Satan was traditionally compared to a whale upon which trusting man moored. So the simile is prophetic of the Fall.'[23] Following up Ricks' suggestion we might note how the 'scaly rinde' of the whale verbally presages the rind of the fruit, and how the compound 'night-founderd' is echoed in the 'night-wanderer' in the simile of further delusion just before the Fall (IX.640); while the 'anchor' is the traditional emblematic anchor of hope which man here misplaces. The simile does more than simply establish Satan's size; the visual image has a wealth of associative connotation.

But reading in this way creates further problems. At the creation we find this account of one of God's creatures:

Leviathan
Hugest of living Creatures, on the Deep

19. Thorpe, *Milton Criticism*, pp. 327-8.
20. *The Common Pursuit*, p. 22.
21. *A Preface to Paradise Lost*, p. 41.
22. B. A. Wright, *Milton's Paradise Lost* (1962), p. 97.
23. Christopher Ricks, *Milton's Grand Style* (1963), p. 6.

> Stretcht like a promontorie sleeps or swimms,
> And seems a moving Land, . . .
>
> (VII.412-415)

The parallel with the earlier passage is close: the whale is stretched out and asleep in each case and looks like land; and there is the verbal echo of 'Hugest'. If we give *Paradise Lost* that kind of close reading Ricks says it requires, the descriptive parallels and verbal echoes in the creation passage will remind us of the description in Book I: so that if man moors unsuspectingly on what is not firm land but is untrustworthy devilry, if Leviathan represents Satan in any way more than in being large in Book I, then these associations are present in Book VII. The Satanic associations of Book I could have been excluded in Book VII by avoiding the name 'Leviathan' and using whale, by not repeating 'Hugest', by avoiding descriptive parallels. Are these echoes and parallels meaningful—or accidental and careless?

If Milton is not careless and the echoes are deliberate, then we have two possible explanations. It can be argued that before the Fall, Leviathan and the serpent are innocent: Milton is saying at creation 'Leviathan (but not—yet—Satan)'; Ricks argues[24] that Milton deliberately uses in an innocent sense words before the Fall that after the Fall have sinful connotations—'error', 'wandring', 'serpent'. On the other hand we might argue that Satan *is* suggested in the Book VII passage, and see this as one of the seemingly recurrent hints of the inevitability of the Fall, or the imminence of it even in innocence. The latter suggestion is one that may make us alter our idea of the 'meaning' of the poem—at the gain of exonerating Milton from charges of vagueness and carelessness.

'Inspired frivolity' was for Eliot a characteristic quality of Milton's similes. The emphasis of recent criticism has been, however, to show how carefully they are organized, to dispel the 'digression' account. An initial point of comparison (like the comparison of the serpent's crest to a will-o'-the-wisp, IX.633ff.) is expanded not into irrelevance but to a wealth of suggestion. Will-o'-the-wisps look like the glowing crest—but the image is not only visual: they also act in such a way as to delude people—just like Satan hidden in the snake; will-o'-the-wisps are English folklore like the elves the devils are compared to (I.781)—examples of error and superstition on Earth, bringing a reminiscence of Hell in at this point, relevantly reminding us of Satan's aims; the night-wanderer is benighted—the night of evil and lack of enlightenment, and the darkness of Hell, metaphors recurrent through the poem; the

24. *Milton's Grand Style*, pp. 109-17.

unctuous vapour is like the mist in which Satan entered Paradise, another of the images of delusion repeated through the poem, like the maze picked up here in 'amaz'd night-wanderer'. And Satan attends the serpent just as 'som evil spirit attends' the *ignis fatuus*. The whole simile is packed with points of relevant comparison, visual and moral, and packed with reference back and forward through the poem.[25]

But just as frequently as similes of comparison we find what Ricks has called the simile of 'ironic disparity'. He points out how Satan (looking at Heaven's gate from the limbo of fools) is compared to Jacob (III.510-525) and earlier in Hell had been compared to Moses (I.338-344)—in each case not from carelessness, but to point out the hideous differences between the evil Satan and the righteous men of God, to show Satan parodying the good.[26]

Again, this is an aspect of the verse that is inseparable from the 'meaning' of the poem. Satan may be a parody of the good, but what is the good when we see God taunting Satan by letting down the stairs to pull them up again, or Moses calling up a locust plague to starve the Egyptians? Does the ironic disparity here, depending as it must on a moral standard, also make an ironic comment on the ways of God?

Apart from his care with individual similes, Milton also created sustained patterns and schemes of imagery, as Broadbent has indicated. In *Revaluation*[27] Leavis compared *Paradise Lost* unfavourably with the 'extended metaphor' of a Shakespearian play. Recent critics, however, have emphasized these related patterns of imagery, the metaphoric organization of *Paradise Lost*. Jackson Cope in *The Metaphoric Structure of 'Paradise Lost'* and Isabel MacCaffrey in *Paradise Lost as 'Myth'* have valuably pointed out the basic metaphoric patterns and structures in the poem. For MacCaffrey the whole poem 'is a great vision of rising and falling action; and in *Paradise Lost* the rise and fall are not only emotional, moral or social, as in tragedy, but literal and topographical as well. Image and meaning are one.'[28] But in addition to this basic metaphor of rising and falling (and we note the fall-rise-high-low-deep-ascend-sink cluster of words) is a second pattern of light-dark imagery. Once again the metaphor is literal in the poem's action (day and night, bright Heaven, and dark Hell) and moral and emotional. It is developed into a greater complexity and richness by word-play:

25. Cf. Addison, *The Spectator*, No. 351 *and* L. Lerner, 'The Miltonic Simile' in *Essays in Criticism*, IV (1954), 306.
26. *Milton's Grand Style*, pp. 127-9.
27. P. 60.
28. Isabel MacCaffrey, *Paradise Lost as 'Myth'* (1959), p. 56.

Cope points out that 'as Satan rises (from the lake) with sparkles of his old light, it is not upon the "*dusky* air" but on "dry Land / He lights" (I.226-228)'.[29] And there is a similar ironic pun on Satan's parodying the moral value of light when at the end of Book III 'on *Niphates* top he lights.' The basic pattern of both these schemes of imagery is given a dynamic richness by punning extensions. And as a further enrichment, the two schemes are involved with each other. The ascent from Hell to Heaven is one from darkness to light; the devils' fall was from light to darkness. Although the two schemes are simple, by their extensions and interrelations they are used with a full poetic richness. And they express, of course, the themes of the poem. The simple moral struggle of evil against good basic to the whole action is presented in the light-dark imagery, and the moral issues arising from this are realized by further metaphors. The contrasts between the order of Heaven and the disorder of Hell are presented by metaphors of order— dance, song, circular movement—contrasting with their opposites— riot, cacophony, semi-circles: volcanoes, whirlwinds, eruptions, barbarian hordes. The productiveness of good and the destructive- ness of evil are similarly presented—by the metaphoric actions of the creation of Earth, and the destructive war in Heaven: and by the further metaphors of the richness of Paradise, evoked by images of fecundity and fertility contrasting with the barrenness of Hell—imaged in wasted plains, ice, deserts, in the windswept Paradise of Fools, and in Paradise after the Flood, when it becomes 'an Iland salt and bare, / The haunt of Seals and Orcs, and Sea mews clang' (XI.834-835). The verse works by a cumulative process. Local effects of punning and suggestion accrete into larger associations; events—the Fall of the Angels—become metaphors; objects—the fruit—become metaphoric by their collected associa- tions; sustained patterns of simile—Satan's voyage, Satan's animal shapes, Eve's gardening and flowers, develop through the poem.

Leavis objected to the verse movement of *Paradise Lost*:

In the end we find ourselves protesting—protesting against the routine gesture, the heavy fall, of the verse, flinching from the foreseen thud that comes so inevitably, and, at last, irresistibly: for reading *Paradise Lost* is a matter of resisting, of standing up against, the verse-movement, of subduing it into something tolerably like sensitiveness, and in the end our resistance is worn down; we surrender at last to the inescapable monotony of the ritual.[30]

29. Jackson Cope, *The Metaphoric Structure of 'Paradise Lost'* (1962), p. 96; Cope's italics.
30. *Revaluation*, pp. 43-4.

Certainly the Miltonic verse paragraph is stylized, certainly it is ritualistic, but it does not follow, as Leavis claims, that by 'cultivating so complete and systematic callousness to the intrinsic nature of English, Milton forfeits all possibility of subtle or delicate life in his verse'.[31] Although Milton's verse movement is not primarily expressive in the way Leavis finds Donne, such expressiveness is created when appropriate. Stein cites passages (e.g. II.249ff.; IX.720ff.) that are in the broken argumentative rhythms of Donne or Greville but, as he emphasizes, 'these passages do not *represent* Milton and they are peripheral to the answerable style because he needed a style he could easily *descend* from, not *rise* from'.[32] But Milton is able to absorb into the grand style this colloquial tone for it is a style that embraces a marvellous variety of manner. It is not all 'magniloquent . . . not doing as much as its impressive pomp and volume seem to be asserting'.[33]

There is, of course, especially in the opening books, magniloquence—'sonorities which are sometimes most enviable', as Ezra Pound said.[34] And it is an appropriate magniloquence for the epic pretence and heroic plans of Hell. Eliot in his first essay on Milton criticized Satan's speech to the angels in Heaven (V.772ff.) because of its

complication deliberately introduced into what was a previously simplified and abstract thought. The dark angel here is not *thinking* or conversing, but making a speech carefully prepared for him; and the arrangement is for the sake of musical value, not for significance . . . the syntax is determined by the musical significance, by the auditory imagination, rather than by the attempt to follow actual speech or thought.[35]

But of course Satan *was* making a speech—and when Eliot goes on to describe this as *rhetoric*, he is quite accurate. The speech was nowhere near to following Satan's thoughts—it was a rhetorical political speech. To criticize rhetoric for possessing rhetorical features seems misguided.

The suggestion was that the whole of *Paradise Lost* was like this. Eliot went on to deplore Milton's departure from conversational speech, and Leavis made a similar comment—'mere orotundity is a disproportionate part of the whole effect'. Both of them were unaccountably unaware of the shifts in style in different episodes. But Louis Martz has pointed out in a brief but valuable account

31. *Revaluation*, p. 53.
32. Stein, *Answerable Style*, p. 133.
33. Leavis, *Revaluation*, p. 46.
34. *Literary Essays of Ezra Pound*, p. 238.
35. 'Milton I' in *On Poetry and Poets*, p. 142.

of 'the various style' how the orotund epic manner of the opening 'is gradually subdued, diminished, and in places almost refined away':[36]

Thus the style of Book IV represents a development out of the highly wrought style of Book I, which now, as one looks back, may seem deliberately overwrought, excessively elaborated, though quite in keeping with its subject, the pretensions of the fallen world. The 'purer air' of Paradise demands a purer style moving out of the high epic manner toward something that at times comes close to a pastoral simplicity, though always enfolded within the epic mode.[37]

In Paradise we have the domestic simplicity of 'no fear lest dinner cool' and the love poetry of Adam and Eve, contrasting with the magnificent rhetoric of the devils, contrasting too with 'the toneless voice of the moral law' in God's speech, contrasting too with the notes of anguish from the narrator—'O much deceived, much failing, hapless *Eve* . . . ' (IX.404ff.). From the sustained periods of the heroic rhetoric we move to the concise staccato speech of God the father, to the circling movements of repetition in Book III—'that be from thee farr, / That farr be from thee, Father' (III.153-154), to the bare simplicity of the final vision of the last two books.

To embrace such variety successfully, the grand style must necessarily have a firm overall structure of manner; and it would be foolish in emphasizing the variety of tone, rhythm and language in the different episodes, to fail to emphasize the peculiar nature of the grand style. It is an amazing creation, with its huge paragraphs, its complex syntax, its patterns of sound; it is indeed artificial, it can indeed be ritualistic, it is always distinctive and individual.

The attack on the style extended beyond issues of language and imagery. It formed the basis for the criticism of the poem's structure and action made by Waldock and Peter. Johnson had complained of the want of human interest and the difficulty of the theme: 'The good and evil of eternity are too ponderous for the wings of wit.'[38] A century later, Bagehot remarked that 'by a curiously fatal error Milton has selected for delineation exactly that part of the Divine nature which is most beyond the reach of the human faculties'.[39] Waldock and Peter revived these objections and found a new basis for them in the attacks on the style. The local vagueness, the carelessness of detail, the dependence on magniloquent assertion, the

36. Louis L. Martz, *The Paradise Within* (1964), p. 117.
37. *The Paradise Within*, p. 119.
38. *Lives of the Poets*, I.216.
39. *Literary Studies* (Everyman's Library, 1911), I.190.

remoteness from colloquial life—all these found parallels in Milton's handling of theme and structure. Waldock argues that Milton created a Satan too attractive and was then forced to degrade him as the poem progressed; he argued, too, that Milton was confused in presenting Adam as falling from human love. While many of Waldock's observations are in part true, he was unwilling to give Milton credit for subtlety or complexity, and unwilling to entertain the idea that Milton intended a tragic tension between Satan's greatness and degradation, between Adam's love for Eve and his duty to God. Empson carried on the 'inconsistencies' approach: but whereas Waldock and Peter had begun with the assumptions that Milton's verse was careless, general, vague, and imprecise, Empson had already demonstrated[40] that it was a finely sensitive, precise and controlled medium and in *Milton's God* although he does not deal with the verse, his arguments are based on his earlier demonstration of its carefulness, suggestiveness, and precision. He reads *Paradise Lost* as a narrative poem in the way Waldock and Peter had done; but his conclusion is that if God seems to lie or contradict himself, if God seems to have complicity in the Fall, that is not evidence of Milton's ineptitude in handling a long narrative poem or a complex theological subject, but a deliberate presentation of character in action, a statement of facts that must be evaluated. The characters in *Paradise Lost* are to be evaluated by the reader like characters in the novel—*all* of them. For Dr Johnson, 'the characters in the *Paradise Lost*, which admit of examination, are those of angels and of man; of angels good and evil; of man in his innocent and sinful state':[41] God did not admit of examination. But for Empson everyone is on trial. *Milton's God* is one of the most exciting and stimulating studies of *Paradise Lost* ever published, and whether or not we agree with its conclusions, the argument it puts forward cannot be ignored, and our view of the poem can never be the same again. The linguistic analysis of the new criticism has led back full circle to Shelley's reading of the poem. It has led, too, to a revival of interest in Milton's argument. In 1967 Dennis Burden's *The Logical Epic* examined Milton's handling of the argument, arguing in opposition to Waldock that Milton was fully aware of the problems of his subject and was at pains to produce a logical account of his theme while at the same time reconciling often apparently contradictory Biblical materials. Burden argues that Milton allowed into his poem an account of Satan and the Fall that questioned, even indicted, God's Providence: however, it was an account presented by Satan or the

40. See *Some Versions of Pastoral* (1935), pp. 149-94.
41. *Lives of the Poets*, I.119.

fallen, and phrased in their distinctive terminology. Milton included this Satanic poem in order to counter—by admitting and then placing—the objections to God's goodness and Providence; and Burden remarks: 'it is only because Milton saw the difficulties of his own thesis that Empson's interpretation seems to me possible'.[42]

The variety of recent criticism of *Paradise Lost* has testified to the variety of the poem. The worst thing we can do is insist on one single approach and, by admitting no other, limit what the poem can offer us. To be willing to accept that it is multi-faceted, that it is a narrative poem, a metaphoric structure, and an argument, a poem of character and of symbolic pattern, a poem of magniloquent grandeur and of domestic simplicity, is to be able to approach and appreciate the huge range of its greatness.

Milton criticism is not static. 'Milton's dislodgment, in the past decade, after his two centuries of predominance, was effected with remarkably little fuss', Leavis began his essay in *Revaluation* (1936).[43] Fortunately, literature cannot be consigned to utter darkness like the fallen angels; no critic possesses God's omnipotence or infallibility. Patrick Murray in his account of twentieth-century criticism of Milton has pointed out the amazing shift in Milton's reputation in the 1930s: 'For the first time since the early eighteenth century it is possible to find many influential accounts of English non-dramatic poetry in which he is given a comparatively minor place, or from which he is altogether excluded.'[44] But already there has been a change. In the last ten years there has been a continual flow of new studies of Milton, offering a wide range of approaches. The dislodgement produced its spate of routine dismissals of *Paradise Lost*—but it also stimulated a re-thinking of the nature of his achievement. The dislodgement produced in reaction a renewal of serious and challenging criticism. The revival in Milton studies now is greater even than the revival in interest in the Metaphysicals that caused his temporary eclipse.

42. Dennis H. Burden, *The Logical Epic* (1967), p. 22n.
43. *Revaluation*, p. 42.
44. Patrick Murray, *Milton: the modern phase* (1967), p. 50.

SELECT BIBLIOGRAPHY

Addison, Joseph, *The Spectator*. Starting with *The Spectator*, No. 267 (5 January 1712) Addison published a series of important essays on *Paradise Lost* on eighteen successive Saturdays. The first six are in Thorpe below. *The Spectator* is available in 4 vols, Everyman Library, and in 5 vols, D. F. Bond (ed.), Oxford 1965.

Barker, Arthur E. (ed.), *Milton—Modern Essays in Criticism*. New York 1965. Thirty-three valuable modern critical essays.

Broadbent, J. B., *Some Graver Subject*. London 1960. Stimulating and suggestive studies of *Paradise Lost*, on both style and argument.

Burden, Dennis H., *The Logical Epic*. London 1967. An invaluable study of the argument, showing Milton's awareness of and handling of his theme's difficulties.

Bush, Douglas, *Paradise Lost in Our Time*. Ithaca, New York 1945. Conservative reading of the poem; defends God against sentimentalists and Satanists.

Cope, Jackson I., *The Metaphoric Structure of 'Paradise Lost'*. Baltimore 1962. Original and rewarding study of metaphorical patterns and structure.

Daniells, Roy, *Milton, Mannerism and Baroque*. Toronto 1963.

Darbishire, Helen, *The Early Lives of Milton*. London 1932. Six illuminating biographies.

Diekhoff, John S., *Milton's Paradise Lost: A Commentary on the Argument*. New York 1946. Christian and conservative account of theme.

Eliot, T. S., 'A Note on the Verse of John Milton' (1936), and 'Milton' (1947) are included in *On Poetry and Poets*, London 1957, as 'Milton I' and 'Milton II'. The latter is abbreviated from its original form, but the full text is available in Thorpe, *Milton Criticism* (1951).

Empson, William, *Some Versions of Pastoral*. London 1935. The American edition is entitled *English Pastoral Poetry*. The essay 'Milton and Bentley' is a brilliant reading of Milton's verse for subtleties of suggestion, implication, ambiguity, and wit.

——, *Milton's God*. London 1961, 2nd edn, London 1965. A major re-examination of *PL*, proposing that Milton was critical of God's motives and behaviour and was indeed a Satanist.

Gardner, Helen, *A Reading of Paradise Lost.* Oxford 1965. Valuable statement of the traditionalist position; Milton's magnificence rather than intellectual or linguistic subtlety.

Grierson, H. J. C., *Milton and Wordsworth: Poets and Prophets.* London 1937. Humane study of Milton as prophetic poet.

Harding, Davis P., *The Club of Hercules: studies in the classical background of Paradise Lost.* Urbana 1962. Useful, informative study.

Johnson, Samuel, *The Rambler*, Nos 86, 88, 90, 92, 94 (1751); 'Life of Milton' in *Lives of the Poets.* World's Classics 1952, Vol. I. *The Rambler* essays are detailed examinations of the versification, language, and style of *Paradise Lost* on which the later generalized criticism of the *Life* is based. Johnson's comments provide a classic statement of the eighteenth-century admiration of the poem, with reservations that still have to be answered by twentieth-century defenders of *Paradise Lost*.

Kermode, Frank (ed.), *The Living Milton.* London 1960. Stimulating collection of original essays.

Leavis, F. R., *Revaluation.* London 1936 and *The Common Pursuit.* London 1952. The three essays in these collections present the major twentieth-century attack, after Eliot, on Milton. Immensely influential in their day, most of their contentions have been countered by the studies of Cope, Empson, MacCaffrey, and Ricks.

Lewis, C. S., *A Preface to Paradise Lost.* London 1942. Necessary reading for its exposition of the epic and hierarchical scheme, less satisfactory on style.

MacCaffrey, Isabel G., *Paradise Lost as 'Myth'.* Cambridge, Mass. 1959. One of the most important studies of the themes, structure and language of *PL*, brilliantly demonstrating its richness.

Martz, Louis L., *The Paradise Within.* New Haven and London 1964. Sensitive insights on variations of style in *PL*, and valuable defence of Books XI and XII. Martz has edited a useful anthology of twelve modern essays, *Milton—Twentieth Century Views.* Englewood Cliffs, N.J. 1966.

Peter, John, *A Critique of Paradise Lost.* London 1960. Provocative and argumentative in Waldock tradition.

Prince, F. T., *The Italian Element in Milton's Verse.* Oxford 1954.

Rajan, B., *Paradise Lost and the Seventeenth Century Reader.* London 1947. Useful study of *PL* in context of seventeenth-century thought and ideas.

Ricks, Christopher, *Milton's Grand Style.* Oxford 1963. Indispensable study of the style showing *PL* sensitive and subtle; convincingly repudiates Leavis/Eliot orthodoxy.

Spaeth, Sigmund, *Milton's Knowledge of Music.* Princeton 1913. Pioneering study of Milton's musical interests with valuable verbal analysis.

Steadman, John M., *Milton and the Renaissance Hero*. Oxford 1967. Documentation of traditional tension between poetic and moral heroism, and of Milton's exploitation of this in presenting Satan and Christ.

Stein, Arnold, *Answerable Style*. Minneapolis 1953. Important and stimulating study of themes and style—particularly on war in Heaven.

Summers, Joseph H., *The Muse's Method*. Cambridge, Mass. 1962.

Thorpe, James (ed.), *Milton Criticism—Selections From Four Centuries*. London 1951. Valuable preface surveying Milton criticism and wide selection of texts.

Tillyard, E. M. W., *Milton*. London 1930; new edn 1966. *The Miltonic Setting*. London 1938. *The Elizabethan World Picture*. London 1943. *Studies in Milton*. London 1951. The first has become a standard commentary on all of Milton's works, the third is an essential study of the background of ideas and beliefs in *PL*.

Waldock, A. J. A., *Paradise Lost and Its Critics*. London 1947. Provocative and important reading of the poem as a narrative; major account of 'inconsistencies', degradation of Satan, etc.

Watkins, W. C. B., *An Anatomy of Milton's Verse*. Baton Rouge 1955.

Wilkes, G. A., *The Thesis of 'Paradise Lost'*. Melbourne 1961; 2nd edn, Sydney 1968. Important account of the thematic structure of good out of evil in *PL*.